Perfectionism

A Step-by-step Approach to Overcoming Perfectionism

(Proven Strategies to End Procrastination, Accept Yourself, and Achieve Your Goals)

Joseph Smith

Published By **Hailey Leigh**

Joseph Smith

All Rights Reserved

Perfectionism: A Step-by-step Approach to Overcoming Perfectionism (Proven Strategies to End Procrastination, Accept Yourself, and Achieve Your Goals)

ISBN 978-1-7382986-5-5

No part of this guidebook shall be reproduced in any form without permission in writing from the publisher except in the case of brief quotations embodied in critical articles or reviews.

Legal & Disclaimer

The information contained in this book is not designed to replace or take the place of any form of medicine or professional medical advice. The information in this book has been provided for educational & entertainment purposes only.

The information contained in this book has been compiled from sources deemed reliable, and it is accurate to the best of the Author's knowledge; however, the Author cannot guarantee its accuracy and validity and cannot be held liable for any errors or omissions. Changes are periodically made to this book. You must consult your doctor or get professional medical advice before using any of the suggested remedies, techniques, or information in this book.

Upon using the information contained in this book, you agree to hold harmless the Author from and against any damages, costs, and expenses, including any legal fees potentially resulting from the application of any of the information provided by this guide. This disclaimer applies to any damages or injury caused by the use and application, whether directly or indirectly, of any advice or information presented, whether for breach of contract, tort, negligence, personal injury, criminal intent, or under any other cause of action.

You agree to accept all risks of using the information presented inside this book. You need to consult a professional medical practitioner in order to ensure you are both able and healthy enough to participate in this program.

Table Of Contents

Chapter 1: Perfection

In our cutting-edge global, the pursuit of perfection regularly seems like a great to strive for—a manner to gather success, reputation, and happiness. But what lies below this apparently noble pursuit? This bankruptcy delves into the multifaceted idea of perfection, its ancient origins, cultural significance, and the mental dynamics that underlie the relentless power to attain it.

Defining Perfection and Its Cultural Significance:

Perfection is a complicated and subjective concept that varies throughout cultures, time durations, and those. At its center, perfection indicates a rustic of flawlessness or of entirety. Yet, this definition can vary significantly depending on context. In artwork, perfection may embody balance and harmony, whilst in a aggressive sports activities placing, perfection ought to endorse achieving the very high-quality rating or fundamental average overall performance degree. This bankruptcy explores the nuances of defining perfection specifically domains and underscores how cultural values shape our understanding of what is ideal.

Historical Context and Evolution:

The roots of the pursuit of perfection can be traced again thru records. Ancient civilizations sought perfection in the form of deities or mythical figures. Philosophers like Plato and Aristotle debated the character of perfection, linking it to ideas of perfect forms and extremely good characteristic. As societies advanced, technological enhancements, industrialization, and mass media contributed to new standards of perfection. The creation of social media has similarly accelerated the ones requirements, amplifying the pressure to give a curated picture of a "super" existence. This financial disaster illuminates how historical contexts have precipitated the concept of perfection and its implications for modern-day-day-day society.

The Allure and Pitfalls of Striving for Perfection:

The enchantment of perfection lies within the promise of achievement, admiration, and success. However, this pursuit regularly comes at a price. Perfectionism, in its extreme bureaucracy, can reason persistent pressure, tension, and burnout. The regular worry of failure, assessment to others, and consistent self-complaint are some of the pitfalls related to the hunt for flawlessness. This bankruptcy examines the paradoxical nature of perfectionism—how it is able to simultaneously pressure achievement and save you nicely-being.

Impact on Mental Health and Well-being:

Perfectionism is carefully intertwined with highbrow health. Research shows that folks who show off immoderate stages of perfectionism are extra liable to tension issues, despair, or maybe suicidal ideation. The consistent want to meet unrealistic requirements takes a toll on emotional properly-being, contributing to a cycle of dissatisfaction and misery. This financial catastrophe delves into the intellectual mechanisms that make a contribution to this terrible effect on mental health.

Cultural Influences and Gender Disparities:

Cultural norms play a big position in shaping beliefs of perfection. Different societies prioritize high-quality trends or behaviors, frequently perpetuating stereotypes and expectancies. Gender additionally performs a important characteristic, as societal expectations concerning appearance, behavior, and success can be extremely awesome for women and men. This financial catastrophe investigates how manner of existence and gender norms engage with the pursuit of perfection, losing moderate at the disparities and worrying conditions confronted via numerous businesses.

The Paradox of Imperfection:

In a worldwide that celebrates innovation, creativity, and improvement, it would appear counterintuitive to speak about imperfection. However, the concept of imperfection is intertwined with our increase as individuals and as a society. Paradoxically, the pursuit of perfection frequently stifles innovation and hampers our potential to adapt to change. By fixating on achieving an impossible terrific, we danger lacking out at the messy, imperfect, but profoundly valuable machine of gaining knowledge of and development. This financial disaster delves into the paradoxical courting amongst perfection and increase, highlighting how embracing imperfection can clearly gasoline improvement.

Media's Role in Perpetuating Perfection:

The upward push of media, in particular social media, has appreciably inspired our perception of perfection. Platforms like Instagram present carefully curated snapshots of people's lives, regularly portraying an idealized version that does not reflect the overall reality. This curated picture can create unrealistic expectancies and make contributions to emotions of inadequacy and envy. The chapter explores the impact of media on our perception of perfection and offers insights into a way to navigate its consequences in a healthy manner.

Perfectionism as a Defense Mechanism:

Perfectionism can every so often feature a defense mechanism—a manner to shield oneself from criticism, rejection, or feelings of inadequacy. By placing impossibly immoderate requirements, human beings create a protecting barrier that guards against vulnerability. However, this protection mechanism can be isolating and destructive to highbrow nicely-being. This financial disaster dives into the intellectual motivations at the back of perfectionism as a protection mechanism, losing moderate on the emotional complexities that stress this conduct.

The Role of Personality Traits:

Personality inclinations play a pivotal feature within the development of perfectionist dispositions. Traits which includes conscientiousness, self-complaint, and neuroticism can make a contribution to the propensity for perfectionism. Additionally, certain tendencies may additionally moreover interact with outside factors to exacerbate or mitigate perfectionist tendencies. This monetary destroy examines the interaction among individual dispositions and perfectionism, providing insights into how the ones tendencies form our courting with the pursuit of perfection.

Perfectionism inside the Workplace:

The place of work is a breeding floor for perfectionism, because the desire to excel and show one's properly properly worth often intersects with professional aspirations. While a exceptional degree of ambition can purpose success, the compulsive need for perfection can result in stress, burnout, and impaired teamwork. This bankruptcy explores the impact of perfectionism on workplace dynamics, average performance, and well-being, in addition to strategies for fostering a extra in shape artwork surroundings.

The Cultivation of Self-Compassion:

Amidst the pressures of perfectionism, self-compassion emerges as a essential antidote. Self-compassion includes treating oneself with the equal kindness and statistics that one would possibly offer to a chum in times of trouble. This financial disaster introduces the concept of self-compassion, its courting to perfectionism, and practical physical sports activities to cultivate self-compassion as a manner to counteract the awful outcomes of perfectionism.

Chapter 2: The Perfectionist Mindset

In the hunt to recognize the psychology of perfection, it's far essential to delve into the complex international of the perfectionist thoughts-set. This chapter explores the nuances of perfectionism, differentiating amongst healthful and bad expressions, figuring out perfectionist tendencies, and analyzing how early reviews shape these tendencies.

Section 2.1: Defining Perfectionism

Perfectionism is a multifaceted concept that consists of placing unrealistically immoderate standards for oneself, observed by way of manner of the use of an unrelenting strain to collect the ones requirements. This mind-set is frequently fueled thru the concern of failure, an unquenchable preference for control, and a strong want for external validation. Perfectionists have a tendency to diploma their self-worth primarily based on their accomplishments and frequently experience tension at the same time as faced with the opportunity of falling quick in their idealized dreams.

Section 2.2: Healthy vs. Unhealthy Perfectionism

While the pursuit of excellence may be motivating and bring about non-public increase, it's miles crucial to distinguish among wholesome and bad perfectionism. Healthy perfectionism entails putting immoderate requirements as a technique of personal increase and improvement. It's related to intrinsic motivation and a enjoy of pride irrespective of the outcome. Unhealthy perfectionism, however, is characterised through rigid necessities, an immoderate worry of failure, and a steady want for approval from others. It can bring about chronic stress, burnout, and horrific influences on intellectual health.

Section 2.Three: Identifying Perfectionist Tendencies

Recognizing perfectionist dispositions inner oneself or others can be a pivotal step closer to expertise this mindset. Common symptoms include setting excessively excessive necessities, feeling distressed even as goals aren't met perfectly, being overly self-crucial, and procrastinating due to fear of now not meeting expectancies. Perfectionists regularly engage in "all-or-now not some thing" thinking, believing that something a good buy much less than perfection is failure.

Section 2.Four: Early Experiences and Development of Perfectionism

Early childhood research play a incredible position within the improvement of perfectionist dispositions. Children who grew up in environments in which achievements have been always rewarded and errors had been no longer tolerated may additionally internalize the perception that fine exquisite universal performance is suitable. Likewise, parental or societal stress to excel can contribute to the formation of perfectionist tendencies. These early studies form the person's middle beliefs approximately their self esteem and the character of achievement.

Section 2.Five: The Role of Fear in Perfectionism

Fear is a driving pressure behind perfectionism, often manifesting as a fear of failure or fear of judgment. Perfectionists may additionally worry that their errors will result in rejection, humiliation, or lack of esteem from others. These fears can motive tension and avoidance behaviors, as human beings try and shield themselves from the possibility of failure.

Section 2.6: Cognitive Patterns and Perfectionism

Perfectionists display off special cognitive styles that perpetuate their mind-set. They normally generally tend to engage in "catastrophic wondering," wherein minor mistakes are blown out of percent, and that they assume dire consequences for even the smallest imperfections. Cognitive distortions, together with "black-and-white wondering" (believing that some component is each ideal or a complete failure) and "need to" statements (enforcing rigid expectations on themselves), make contributions to the depth of perfectionism.

Section 2.7: The Link Between Perfectionism and Self-Esteem

Perfectionists regularly tie their self confidence to their achievements and the manner properly they meet their personal unrealistic requirements. As a stop result, their shallowness becomes contingent on outside validation and perfect performance. This link amongst perfectionism and vanity can create a by no means-finishing cycle of looking for approval and struggling to maintain an photo of perfection, important to persistent stress and anxiety.

Section 2.Eight: Perfectionism and Imposter Syndrome

Imposter Syndrome, a phenomenon wherein individuals doubt their accomplishments and worry being exposed as "frauds," frequently is going hand in hand with perfectionism. Perfectionists regularly characteristic their successes to outdoor factors which incorporates right fortune, while internalizing their failures as inherent flaws. This self-sabotaging cycle further reinforces their feelings of inadequacy and fuels the need to constantly attempt for now not possible levels of perfection.

Section 2.Nine: Perfectionism and Comparison

In modern hyperconnected worldwide, the prevalence of social media exacerbates the perfectionist mind-set. Perfectionists frequently take a look at themselves to others, focusing on the achievements and seemingly flawless lives portrayed on-line. This regular social evaluation intensifies emotions of inadequacy, fuels the selection to maintain up, and contributes to a awful self-photo.

Section 2.10: Perfectionism and Procrastination

Paradoxically, perfectionism can bring about procrastination. The fear of not assembly excessive requirements may additionally moreover create masses strain that individuals delay beginning a project altogether. The tension approximately not being able to achieve perfection can emerge as so overwhelming that it will become much less complicated to avoid the assignment altogether in choice to stand functionality failure.

Section 2.Eleven: Perfectionism and Relationships

The perfectionist mindset may also have profound implications on private relationships. Unrealistic expectations and a ordinary need for validation can pressure relationships, as pals and own family may additionally experience not able to satisfy the perfectionist's necessities. This can bring about emotions of frustration, isolation, and misunderstandings, because the perfectionist's conduct is often pushed with the aid of the usage of tension and an insatiable quest for perfection.

Section 2.12: Cultivating Self-Compassion

Shifting from a perfectionist mind-set to a healthier perspective requires cultivating self-compassion. Self-compassion includes treating oneself with the same kindness and records that one could possibly provide to a pal. It recognizes that errors are a natural part of being human and enables human beings reframe their perception of failure. By training self-compassion, perfectionists can progressively launch themselves from the grip of unrealistic requirements and fear of imperfection.

Section 2.Thirteen: Seeking Professional Help

For the ones grappling with the greater excessive components of perfectionism, searching out expert help is a important step. Therapists, counselors, and psychologists can offer guidance in unraveling deep-seated ideals, addressing cognitive distortions, and studying practical techniques to manage perfectionist tendencies. Cognitive-behavioral remedy (CBT), mindfulness techniques, and arrogance constructing sports can be powerful device in this adventure.

Section 2.14: Embracing Growth Mindset

Transitioning from a fixed mindset to a growth thoughts-set may be transformative for perfectionists. A increase thoughts-set emphasizes that abilties and traits may be superior via effort, studying, and resilience. Embracing a boom thoughts-set lets in people to understand disturbing conditions as possibilities for boom in desire to threats to their self confidence, fostering a more healthy approach to accomplishing personal excellence.

Section 2.15: Conclusion

The perfectionist mind-set, with its roots in excessive necessities, worry of failure, and unyielding pursuit of control, is a highbrow labyrinth that influences severa aspects of an character's lifestyles. From the manner it shapes arrogance and relationships to its hyperlink with imposter syndrome and procrastination, perfectionism's have an impact on is a protracted way-achieving and frequently unfavourable to intellectual properly-being. However, this financial ruin moreover highlights that perfectionism is not a hard and fast u . S .; it's miles a mind-set that may be understood, challenged, and converted.

Recognizing the signs and symptoms and signs and symptoms of perfectionism, facts its origins, and acknowledging its impact is the first step towards trade. As human beings cultivate self-compassion, encompass a increase mind-set, and are seeking out expert help if essential, they may be capable of often launch themselves from the suffocating grip of perfectionism. This transformation opens the door to a more balanced and suitable existence—one that values development over perfection, embraces imperfection as a natural a part of being human, and celebrates the journey of boom and self-discovery.

In the subsequent chapters, we are able to maintain to find out the multifaceted nature of perfectionism, its have an effect on on on severa elements of our lives, and the strategies to interrupt loose from its constraints. Through understanding, introspection, and practical movement, humans can navigate the complicated terrain of the perfectionist mind-set and embark on a adventure of private growth and properly-being.

The Illusion of Control

Chapter three delves into the idea of manipulate within the context of perfectionism. Control frequently performs a large role in the lives of perfectionists, impacting their behavior, emotions, and contemporary properly-being. This bankruptcy explores the underlying intellectual mechanisms, cognitive biases, and results of looking for control in severa factors of lifestyles.

Section 1: The Need for Control

1.1 Understanding Control:

The financial ruin starts offevolved offevolved through the usage of using explaining the idea of manage and its importance in human psychology. Control refers to the capability to influence effects, control situations, and revel in a experience of mastery over events. Perfectionists regularly gravitate in the course of control as a way to restriction uncertainty, lessen tension, and preserve a revel in of order.

1.2 Control and Perfectionism:

This subsection examines the difficult dating amongst manage and perfectionism. It highlights how the want for manipulate can pressure perfectionist behaviors, which incorporates meticulous planning, inflexible exercising routines, and immoderate interest on information. The desire for manage can stem from a worry of imperfection and failure, essential perfectionists to trying to find control over their environment and usual overall performance.

Section 2: Cognitive Biases and Control

2.1 Illusion of Control Bias:

One cognitive bias explored on this segment is the "phantasm of control" bias. This bias leads human beings to overestimate their capability to govern outcomes, even in conditions wherein manage is minimum or nonexistent. Perfectionists might exhibit this bias with the aid of believing that their efforts can prevent horrible consequences, even when external elements play a big characteristic.

2.2 Confirmation Bias and Control:

Confirmation bias, the tendency to look for and interpret statistics that confirms preexisting ideals, can deliver a boost to the illusion of manage. Perfectionists also can interest on instances wherein their efforts reason terrific consequences, reinforcing their notion that manage is powerful.

Section three: Control and Anxiety

3.1 Control and Anxiety Relationship:

This subsection delves into the effect of manage on tension. While the pursuit of control goals to reduce tension, it regularly paradoxically will growth anxiety due to the strain to maintain unrealistic requirements. Perfectionists can also experience heightened anxiety when they apprehend a loss of manage or stumble upon situations wherein they can't hold their desired diploma of precision.

Chapter 3: Fear Of Failure

Introduction:

The worry of failure is a powerful psychological strain that underlies many components of perfectionism. This chapter delves into the origins of this fear, its impact on people, and techniques to manipulate and conquer it.

Section 1: Understanding the Fear of Failure

1.1 The Psychological Roots:

The worry of failure often originates from youth reviews, wherein mistakes could have been met with complaint or punishment. Such stories can bring about a deep-seated fear of no longer meeting expectancies, generating tension and avoidance behaviors.

1.2 Perceived Consequences:

Perfectionists will be inclined to catastrophize the capability effects of failure, imagining extreme consequences. This heightened worry of the worst-case state of affairs magnifies the tension round making errors.

1.3 The Vicious Cycle:

The fear of failure feeds into perfectionism, as people strive to keep away from mistakes the least bit fees. However, this cycle is counterproductive, major to procrastination, overthinking, and paralysis due to the overpowering strain to prevail.

Section 2: Differentiating Fear of Failure from Fear of Success

2.1 Fear of Success:

Interestingly, perfectionism is not absolutely pushed through way of fear of failure; it's also fueled through the use of the fear of success. Success might entail accelerated expectations, extra duties, and the pressure to constantly meet immoderate standards, which may be daunting.

2.2 Balancing Both Fears:

Understanding the dual nature of those fears is crucial. Identifying which fear is extra dominant for an individual can help tailor interventions that deal with precise factors of their perfectionism.

Section three: Strategies to Address Fear of Failure

three.1 Embracing Imperfection:

Encouraging humans to reframe failure as a stepping stone to increase can lessen the grip of worry. Emphasizing that perfection isn't always viable and that setbacks are herbal can reduce the depth of the concern.

3.2 Setting Realistic Goals:

Assisting perfectionists in placing potential desires reduces the threat of failure and the related fear. Breaking down larger obligations into capability steps can alleviate overwhelming strain.

three.Three Reframing the Consequences:

Helping individuals reevaluate the capability consequences of failure can reduce anxiety. Exploring the real effects and their effect on prolonged-time period desires can offer a extra balanced mindset.

3.Four Building Resilience:

Teaching resilience capabilities complements an person's functionality to cope with setbacks. Learning the way to get higher, adapt, and take a look at from disasters can reduce the fear's electricity over their actions.

Section four: Self-Compassion as a Counterbalance

4.1 Practicing Self-Compassion:

Encouraging self-compassion involves treating oneself with the equal kindness and knowledge one would possibly provide to a pal. This counteracts the merciless self-criticism that often accompanies worry of failure.

4.2 Recognizing Common Humanity:

Helping perfectionists recognize that everyone memories failure is vital. Understanding that failure is ordinary reduces emotions of isolation and shame.

four.Three Mindfulness and Acceptance:

Mindfulness techniques domesticate present-2d reputation, permitting human beings to detach from their fears and anxieties. Accepting their fears with out judgment permits reduce their hold on one's mind and moves.

Section 5: Overcoming Fear of Failure in Practice

5.1 Exposure Therapy:

Gradual publicity to situations that purpose the fear of failure can help desensitize people over the years. Starting with small worrying situations and progressively growing the hassle can assemble self assure in coping with setbacks.

5.2 Cognitive Restructuring:

Identifying and tough awful notion patterns associated with failure is critical. Helping people replace self-restricting ideals with more practical and balanced mind can lessen the intensity of the priority.

5.Three Positive Self-Talk:

Encouraging super self-communicate can counteract the self-vital internal speak that fuels the priority of failure. Teaching humans to reframe terrible thoughts into keeping statements can shift their mind-set.

Section 6: Parental and Societal Influences

6.1 Parental Expectations:

Exploring how parental expectancies make contributions to the improvement of the fear of failure is essential. Children raised with unrealistic requirements are more likely to internalize a fear of disappointing others.

6.2 Academic and Social Pressure:

Societal pressures to excel academically, professionally, and socially can exacerbate the fear of failure. Understanding cultural affects and hard unrealistic societal requirements are critical for coping with this worry.

6.Three The Role of Failure in Learning:

Educating parents, teachers, and caregivers approximately the function of failure in analyzing is crucial. Fostering an environment that embraces mistakes as opportunities for boom can mitigate the improvement of a paralyzing worry of failure.

Section 7: Professional Support and Intervention

7.1 Therapeutic Approaches:

Psychological remedies like cognitive-behavioral treatment (CBT) can correctly deal with the fear of failure. Therapists art work with individuals to select out idea patterns, reframe ideals, and broaden coping strategies.

7.2 Mindfulness-Based Interventions:

Mindfulness practices help human beings take a look at their thoughts and feelings without judgment. These strategies can lessen the tension related to the priority of failure, selling a extra balanced attitude.

7.Three Support Groups:

Joining aid groups for people suffering with perfectionism can provide a experience of community and shared knowledge. Hearing others' tales and coping strategies may be immensely reassuring.

Section 8: Navigating Fear of Failure in Different Contexts

eight.1 Fear of Failure within the Workplace:

Addressing how the concern of failure influences venture regular performance and profession development is essential. Strategies together with trying to find comments, placing easy dreams, and acknowledging accomplishments can counteract this worry.

8.2 Fear of Failure in Relationships:

Discussing the effect of the priority of failure on non-public relationships is critical. Open communication, placing realistic expectancies, and cultivating emotional vulnerability can foster more healthy connections.

eight.Three Fear of Failure in Personal Goals:

Exploring how the concern of failure impacts the pursuit of personal desires, pastimes, and pastimes is important. Encouraging humans to set desires for intrinsic delight in preference to external validation can alleviate the priority's have an impact on.

Conclusion:

In give up, the concern of failure is a pervasive strain that drives many additives of perfectionism. It originates from a aggregate of adolescence research, societal pressures, and internalized ideals. This worry frequently creates a paralyzing cycle of avoidance, self-criticism, and procrastination, hindering private and expert growth.

However, the adventure to overcome the concern of failure isn't always insurmountable. By recognizing that failure is a herbal part of the getting to know way and embracing imperfection, people can shift their mindset. Setting realistic dreams, training resilience, and cultivating self-compassion counteract the debilitating effects of this worry.

Furthermore, interventions like exposure treatment, cognitive restructuring, and mindfulness strategies provide sensible equipment to confront and manipulate the priority of failure. Seeking professional manual, whether or not via treatment or assist agencies, can provide guidance and validation for the ones navigating this difficult journey.

Ultimately, breaking unfastened from the grip of the concern of failure includes a shift in mind-set and a willingness to embody vulnerability. Accepting that setbacks are not synonymous with personal inadequacy empowers humans to pursue their dreams with renewed enthusiasm. By operating thru this fear, people can foster a extra healthy relationship with achievement, analyzing, and their very private self-worth. In the following chapters, we're capable of hold to explore the complex layers of perfectionism and its mental implications, offering insights and strategies to persuade a greater balanced and pleasant existence.

External Validation and Self-Worth

In this monetary wreck, we delve into the complex dating among perfectionism, outside validation, and self confidence. We discover how the steady need for approval and reputation from others can shape one's self-concept and make contributions to the development of perfectionist tendencies. We moreover offer techniques to domesticate inner validation and assemble a healthful revel in of self esteem.

Section 1: The Perfectionism-Validation Connection

We start via dissecting the robust connection amongst perfectionism and the search for outside validation. Perfectionists regularly tie their self esteem to the critiques and remarks of others, most important to a cycle of seeking out affirmation via achievements. We delve into the highbrow reasons behind this conduct, citing research that show how societal expectations and comparisons play a function in driving this need for approval.

Section 2: The Impact on Self-Worth and Identity

In this phase, we discover the consequences of depending carefully on outdoor validation for self confidence. We speak how this reliance can bring about a delicate enjoy of identity, in which one's value becomes contingent on ordinary fulfillment and approval. The toll of this cycle on highbrow fitness is referred to, which encompass stepped forward tension, self-doubt, and despair.

Section three: Strategies for Cultivating Internal Validation

To counteract the horrific consequences of attempting to find external validation, we present severa strategies for nurturing inner validation. These techniques encompass:

1. Mindfulness Practices: We talk how mindfulness can help human beings detach their self confidence from outdoor reviews, permitting them to interest on the existing second and their non-public intrinsic price.

2. Self-Compassion Techniques: Introducing self-compassion practices to deal with oneself with kindness, even inside the face of failure, can wreck the cycle of seeking out validation from others.

3. Identifying Core Values: Helping readers find out and prioritize their middle values lets in them to define their self-worth based totally totally on private mind in desire to out of doors measures.

4. Journaling for Self-Reflection: Encouraging journaling physical sports that sell self-pondered photograph and self-confirmation can resource in constructing a immoderate nice self-photo.

Section four: Navigating Relationships

This segment addresses how perfectionism's impact on outdoor validation influences relationships. We speak the worrying situations of retaining actual connections even as one's self esteem is tied to approval-searching for behavior. We furthermore provide verbal exchange techniques to foster healthier interactions, together with open talk approximately feelings and expectancies.

Section 5: Balancing Validation and Authenticity

In the final section, we consciousness at the importance of locating a balance amongst searching out validation and staying true to oneself. We discover situations wherein outside validation may be useful, which includes effective comments, at the identical time as emphasizing the importance of preserving authenticity and staying aligned with one's values.

Section 6: Overcoming the Fear of Disapproval

One of the underlying drivers of searching out outdoor validation is the fear of disapproval or rejection. In this section, we delve into the origins of this worry and the way it can make a contribution to perfectionist tendencies. We speak the function of past recollections and societal pressures in shaping this worry and offer strategies to overcome it:

1. Reframing Negative Feedback: Encouraging readers to view grievance as an possibility for growth in place of a meditated picture of their surely well really worth can help mitigate the concern of disapproval.

2. Constructive Self-Talk: Introducing readers to strategies of effective and keeping self-speak can empower them to counteract

horrific ideals that strain the priority of disapproval.

3. Gradual Exposure: Gradually exposing oneself to conditions that cause the worry of disapproval, in a managed and supportive manner, can help desensitize the emotional response.

Chapter 4: Relationships And Social Impact

Perfectionism's Effects on Personal Relationships:

Perfectionism has a ways-achieving results that boom past an character's private desires and aspirations. In this bankruptcy, we're going to delve into the complicated ways wherein perfectionism can impact relationships, each with friends and own family, similarly to in romantic partnerships.

1. Communication Challenges and Unrealistic Expectations:

Perfectionist humans regularly war with effective communique because of their tendency to set unrealistically excessive requirements for themselves and others. These unrealistic expectations can result in frustration, as they will perceive any moderate deviation from those ideals as a failure. This can result in trouble expressing wishes and concerns, as well as a reluctance to accept remarks.

2. Fear of Vulnerability:

Perfectionism can be fueled with the useful resource of a worry of vulnerability. People who fear being visible as imperfect may additionally additionally keep away from sharing their real mind and feelings, main to a lack of emotional intimacy in their relationships. This worry of vulnerability can avoid the improvement of deep connections and save you the formation of right bonds.

3. Strain on Emotional Well-being:

The relentless pursuit of perfection can lead to chronic strain, tension, or maybe depression. These emotional states can impact one's interactions with others, causing them to seem faraway, irritable, or withdrawn. Friends and loved ones may additionally moreover furthermore battle to recognize the underlying reasons for those emotional shifts.

Navigating Perfectionism in Different Relationship Contexts:

1. Family Dynamics:

Perfectionism regularly originates from circle of relatives dynamics, collectively with parental expectancies and conditional love. Children who broaden up feeling that their well well worth is tied to their achievements also can develop perfectionist inclinations. This financial ruin explores the cycle of perfectionism in households, how it's perpetuated, and how it could be disrupted thru open communique, placing realistic expectancies, and fostering unconditional love.

2. Friendships:

Perfectionism can complicate friendships by using way of introducing opposition and assessment. Perfectionists may also moreover furthermore examine their achievements to those of their pals and conflict with feelings of inadequacy or jealousy. We speak strategies for nurturing healthful friendships, together with open verbal exchange, empathy, and knowledge that everyone's adventure is particular.

three. Romantic Relationships:

Perfectionism can location sizeable strain on romantic partnerships. Individuals can also worry revealing their imperfections to their associate, leading to an loss of capability to clearly be a part of on an emotional diploma. The financial ruin explores how couples can navigate perfectionism through fostering open conversations, putting practical expectancies, and prioritizing emotional intimacy.

4. Conflict Resolution:

Perfectionists can also find out it hard to cope with conflicts constructively, as they'll understand disagreements as proof of failure or inadequacy. The bankruptcy gives techniques for powerful conflict desire, which includes active listening, empathetic communication, and specializing in answers in area of blame.

5. Cultivating Self-Compassion:

A important subject matter on this bankruptcy is the importance of cultivating self-compassion. By gaining knowledge of to deal with oneself with kindness and know-how, people can wreck the cycle of attempting to find out of doors validation and reduce the effect of perfectionism on their relationships. Self-compassion lets in people to technique themselves and others with empathy, fostering greater healthy and in addition quality connections.

Navigating Perfectionism in Different Relationship Contexts (continued):

6. Supportive Strategies for Partners:

Partners of perfectionists play a crucial role in assisting their cherished ones thru their perfectionist dispositions. The chapter discusses the importance of endurance, empathy, and energetic listening. Partners can encourage open talk approximately perfectionism, offer reassurance, and help create a secure region in which imperfections are regularly taking place and valued.

7. Setting Boundaries:

Perfectionists may additionally moreover struggle with placing limitations in relationships, often feeling obligated to satisfy others' expectancies on the rate in their personal well-being. This monetary disaster explores the significance of setting up wholesome boundaries and setting forward one's goals without fear of rejection. Learning to mention "no" and prioritize self-care is critical in keeping fulfilling relationships.

8. Encouraging Authenticity:

Creating an environment that encourages authenticity is critical in navigating perfectionism inside relationships. Individuals can discover ways to consist of vulnerability and honesty, main to deeper connections and a experience of shared humanity. We find out sports activities activities and conversation strategies that foster authenticity and mutual understanding.

nine. Overcoming Comparison and Jealousy:

Perfectionists can also conflict with evaluating themselves to others, essential to feelings of jealousy or inadequacy. The economic disaster delves into strategies for overcoming those inclinations, which include practicing gratitude, that specialize in private increase, and reframing comparisons as opportunities for notion in desire to belongings of negativity.

10. Mindful Presence in Relationships:

Mindfulness may be a effective device for counteracting the terrible outcomes of perfectionism in relationships. By practising present-2d hobby, people can lessen tension approximately the future and regrets approximately the beyond. This permits them to engage extra truly with their cherished ones, enhancing emotional connections and common courting delight.

11. Seeking Professional Help:

For individuals whose perfectionism extensively impacts their relationships and properly-being, on the lookout for professional assistance is essential. Therapists and counselors can provide steering, offering coping strategies and equipment tailor-made to character desires. The chapter discusses the blessings of therapy and gives insights into severa restoration techniques that may be powerful in addressing perfectionism-related demanding situations.

12. Support Groups and Community:

Perfectionism can regularly make human beings feel remoted and by myself. Engaging with manual groups, each in-individual and on-line, can provide a experience of network and validation. The financial ruin explores the blessings of connecting with others who percentage comparable critiques, supplying a platform for sharing memories, in search of advice, and constructing a aid community.

Conclusion

By acknowledging imperfections, embracing vulnerability, and valuing authenticity, people can create relationships that thrive however the pressures of perfectionism. As we've got explored in this economic disaster, perfectionism's effect on relationships may be profound, affecting verbal exchange, emotional intimacy, and conflict choice. However, armed with records and strategies, people can navigate the challenges posed via perfectionism and foster extra healthful, more pleasant connections.

Remember that progress is fundamental. Overcoming perfectionism inside relationships is a journey that calls for endurance and strive. By adopting a growth mind-set and committing to continuous self-development, humans can step by step dismantle the restrictions that perfectionism erects and replace them with bridges of records, empathy, and assist.

In the imminent chapters, we are able to delve deeper into unique strategies and interventions which can help individuals damage unfastened from the clutches of perfectionism. From cognitive-behavioral techniques to mindfulness practices, each tool contributes to a whole toolkit for overcoming perfectionism and cultivating a lifestyles rich with tremendous connections and personal boom.

As we flow into forward, hold in thoughts that the adventure to extra healthful relationships and self-recognition is a device, no longer an right away transformation. By embracing imperfections and mastering to love oneself and others with authenticity, compassion, and empathy, humans can gather relationships that aren't most effective strong however additionally nurturing, resilient, and emotionally fun.

Performance and Achievement

In this chapter, we delve into the tricky courting amongst perfectionism and normal

normal overall performance, examining how the pursuit of perfection can every encourage and limit personal achievement. We find out the nuanced variations between striving for excellence and the frequently unrealistic pursuit of flawlessness. Additionally, we deal with the terrible consequences of typical overall performance tension and burnout that perfectionism can exacerbate. Through practical strategies and insights, readers will discover ways to set realistic dreams, manipulate expectancies, and foster a greater healthy technique to project their aspirations.

Section 1: The Pursuit of Excellence vs. Perfection

This section begins offevolved by means of using distinguishing among the pursuit of excellence, characterised thru putting excessive requirements and searching for non-stop development, and the pursuit of perfection, which includes unrealistic and unbelievable requirements. We talk how perfectionism can result in procrastination, as people fear now not assembly their unbelievable goals. Case research and real-lifestyles examples illustrate the evaluation amongst healthful striving and the pitfalls of perfectionism.

Section 2: Performance Anxiety and Burnout

In this segment, we have a examine the heightened performance anxiety skilled with the resource of perfectionists. The fear of making mistakes and not assembly their non-public impossibly excessive necessities frequently ends in expanded pressure and tension. We discover the physiological and mental influences of persistent stress, collectively with burnout, that could end end result from extended perfectionistic dispositions. The speak additionally touches on the vicious cycle of perfectionism: the extra humans try for perfection, the more pressured they emerge as, primary to reduced performance.

Section three: Setting Realistic Goals

Here, we introduce the idea of putting SMART goals (Specific, Measurable, Achievable, Relevant, Time-positive) as a way to counteract the terrible elements of perfectionism. We offer practical steps to break down massive goals into potential obligations and milestones. By focusing on improvement in desire to a rigid endpoint, readers can reduce the overwhelming stress that perfectionism regularly imposes. Case research show how people who shift their interest to viable desires experience progressed motivation and satisfaction.

Section four: Embracing Progress Over Perfection

This phase explores the idea of embracing a boom mind-set, wherein effort and studying are prioritized over ideal effects. We talk the importance of acknowledging mistakes and setbacks as opportunities for boom and learning. By reframing disasters as stepping stones rather than signs of inadequacy, humans can build resilience and broaden a greater in form courting with their achievements. Practical sporting activities encourage readers to reevaluate their perceptions of achievement and redefine what it method to make progress.

Section five: Cultivating Self-Compassion

We delve into the characteristic of self-compassion as an antidote to perfectionism. Self-compassion consists of treating oneself with the identical kindness and understanding as one would possibly offer to a chum managing demanding conditions. Through guided wearing sports, readers learn how to understand their inner critic and update it with self-compassionate self-communicate. This section additionally addresses the tendency for perfectionists to have interaction in awful self-talk, and offers techniques to reframe the ones detrimental notion patterns.

Section 6: Strategies for Managing Performance Anxiety

Practical strategies to control fashionable overall performance tension are mentioned in this section. Techniques which include deep respiratory, visualization, and mindfulness are explored as equipment to lessen pressure and anxiety earlier than and during excessive-pressure situations. Readers benefit insights into how schooling, realistic self-appraisal, and that specialize inside the triumphing 2nd can alleviate the paralyzing outcomes of perfectionism-driven anxiety.

Section 7: Balancing Self-Worth and Achievement

The very last phase facilities on the relationship amongst self-worth and achievements. We discover how perfectionism can cause conditional vanity, in which an character's self-worth is tied completely to their accomplishments. By fostering a revel in of intrinsic charge and worthiness, readers can detach their conceitedness from outdoor validation and enjoy a greater stable enjoy of self. Personal anecdotes and sporting occasions guide readers via the system of nurturing self-worth independently of their achievements.

Section eight: Mindful Performance and Flow States

This segment explores the thoughts of mindfulness and flow states as powerful system for managing perfectionism and improving preferred performance. Mindfulness practices encourage people to stay truly gift and engaged inside the task to hand, decreasing preoccupation with perfectionist troubles. Flow states, characterized through intense focus and immersion, allow humans to enjoy a enjoy of timelessness and reachable movement, minimizing the disruptive outcomes of self-doubt and overthinking.

Chapter 5: Cognitive Patterns And Self-Talk

In this financial disaster, we delve deep into the cognitive patterns and self-communicate that underlies the psychology of perfectionism. We discover the complicated approaches wherein our mind and inner dialogues shape our perceptions of ourselves and the arena spherical us. By facts and tough the ones styles, we're capable of start to interrupt unfastened from the grip of perfectionism and domesticate more wholesome mindsets.

Section 1: The Anatomy of Perfectionist Thinking

We start by the use of the usage of dissecting the commonplace cognitive styles that perfectionists often engage in. These styles perpetuate unrealistic requirements and self-complaint, fostering a vicious cycle of in no manner feeling nicely sufficient. Key cognitive distortions include:

1. All-or-Nothing Thinking: The tendency to view subjects in severe terms, in which consequences are both ideal or popular disasters.

2. Overgeneralization: Drawing tremendous conclusions based totally mostly on constrained reviews, along with believing that one failure manner you may always fail.

3. Catastrophizing: Magnifying small setbacks into catastrophic events, amplifying stress and anxiety.

4. Personalization: Taking obligation for outside sports which might be beyond one's manipulate, predominant to unwarranted self-blame.

Section 2: The Power of Self-Talk

We find out the concept of self-speak, the internal communicate that shapes our feelings and behaviors. Perfectionists regularly have a harsh and essential self-communicate that perpetuates their unrealistic standards. We delve into two primary forms of self-talk:

1. Negative Self-Talk: Identifying and addressing the self-defeating language that fuels perfectionism.

2. Positive Self-Talk: Cultivating compassionate and sensible self-speak that promotes boom and self-popularity.

Section three: Cognitive-Behavioral Strategies for Change

In this section, we equip readers with realistic strategies to task and rework their cognitive patterns and self-communicate. These techniques are rooted in cognitive-behavioral treatment (CBT) mind:

1. Identify Cognitive Distortions: Encouraging readers to emerge as privy to unique cognitive distortions they have interaction in, and recognizing how the ones distortions impact their feelings and moves.

2. Reality Testing: Guiding readers to significantly take a look at their thoughts with the resource of the use of looking for evidence for and in the direction of their beliefs. This lets in in reducing black-and-white thinking.

three. Alternative Explanations: Encouraging readers to generate possibility reasons for situations, promoting a more balanced perspective that considers more than one factors.

4. Thought Records: Introducing the exercising of keeping notion records, in which readers file bad thoughts, the triggering conditions, feelings, and opportunity viewpoints.

five. Socratic Questioning: Teaching readers to ask probing inquiries to undertaking and reframe horrible thoughts, number one to greater rational and balanced questioning.

Section four: Mindfulness and Perfectionism

We find out the location of mindfulness in handling perfectionism. Mindfulness practices help individuals have a study their thoughts without judgment, fostering self-attention and decreasing automated reactions. Mindfulness strategies embody:

1. Breath Awareness: Teaching readers to interest on their breath to anchor their interest, that could assist manipulate anxiety and growth self-law.

2. Body Scan: Guiding readers through a frame experiment meditation to make bigger consciousness of physical sensations and reduce tension associated with perfectionist inclinations.

three. Thought Observation: Encouraging readers to test their thoughts as passing intellectual activities, in preference to as correct reflections of truth.

Section five: Integrating Self-Compassion

We emphasize the significance of self-compassion in the adventure inside the route of overcoming perfectionism. Self-compassion consists of treating oneself with the identical kindness and information one would possibly offer to a pal. Key factors of self-compassion encompass:

1. Self-Kindness: Encouraging readers to be slight and know-how within the course of themselves, particularly in moments of failure or struggle.

2. Common Humanity: Reminding readers that imperfection is a shared human revel in and that everyone faces traumatic situations and setbacks.

3. Mindfulness: Incorporating mindfulness practices into self-compassion to foster gift-2d popularity and decrease self-complaint.

Section 6: Implementing Change in Daily Life

Moving beforehand, we talk realistic strategies readers can enforce the strategies included inside the monetary smash into their each day lives:

1. Journaling Exercises: Encouraging readers to hold a magazine where they tune their cognitive distortions, venture terrible mind, and file development through the years. This workout fosters self-awareness and accountability.

2. Positive Affirmations: Introducing the idea of powerful affirmations, in which readers create and repeat setting forward statements that counteract terrible self-talk. This enables to rewire neural pathways related to self-complaint.

three. Gratitude Practice: Guiding readers to cultivate a each day gratitude exercise, wherein they hobby on appreciating their efforts, achievements, and the excessive first-rate factors in their lives.

four. Setting Realistic Goals: Emphasizing the significance of putting potential dreams, breaking massive responsibilities into smaller steps, and celebrating every milestone reached.

Section 7: Overcoming Setbacks and Relapses

We broadly diagnosed that setbacks and relapses are a natural a part of the adventure to overcoming perfectionism. We offer guidance on the manner to deal with the ones moments:

1. Self-Compassion in Setbacks: Encouraging readers to reply to setbacks with self-compassion rather than self-criticism. This entails acknowledging troubles and supplying oneself kindness.

2. Learning from Relapses: Highlighting the gaining knowledge of opportunities that come from relapses. Readers are encouraged to mirror on triggers and coping techniques to decorate their resilience.

Section eight: Seeking Professional Support

Recognizing that overcoming perfectionism may be hard, we communicate the advantages of seeking out expert help:

1. Therapy Options: Introducing readers to cognitive-behavioral remedy (CBT) and mindfulness-primarily based remedies as effective procedures to address perfectionism.

2. Therapist Collaboration: Encouraging readers to collaborate with therapists in placing realistic dreams, gaining expertise of new coping techniques, and exploring the inspiration motives of their perfectionist dispositions.

Section 9: Building a Support System

We emphasize the importance of building a resource system to navigate the journey a long way from perfectionism:

1. Friends and Family: Suggesting techniques to speak one's struggles to loved ones, fostering knowledge and garnering emotional aid.

2. Support Groups: Introducing the idea of assist corporations or on line groups wherein

people can hook up with others who're on a similar adventure.

Section 10: Celebrating Progress

Lastly, we talk the significance of celebrating development, regardless of how small:

1. Self-Appreciation Rituals: Encouraging readers to set up rituals that bear in mind their achievements, reinforcing the concept that improvement is a series of small steps.

2. Reflection and Growth: Guiding readers to periodically mirror on their adventure, acknowledging how a long way they have got come and figuring out regions for persevered growth.

Section 11: Applying Cognitive Strategies in Real-Life Scenarios

In this segment, we provide readers with actual-lifestyles situations and display a manner to take a look at the cognitive techniques blanketed in advance:

1. Scenario 1: A Presentation Gone Wrong

Readers are furnished with a state of affairs in which a perfectionist's presentation failed to bypass as planned.

We manual them via figuring out horrible self-speak, cognitive distortions, and possibility motives.

Readers discover ways to reframe the scenario and understand their efforts regardless of the very last consequences.

2. Scenario 2: Comparing Achievements

Readers are provided with a state of affairs wherein a perfectionist continuously compares their achievements to others'.

We help them exercise mindfulness thru the usage of observing their mind with out judgment and spotting the not unusual humanity in experiencing self-doubt.

3. Scenario 3: Fear of Making Mistakes

Readers encounter a situation in which a perfectionist is paralyzed with the resource of the usage of the priority of creating mistakes.

We manual them thru truth checking out, encouraging them to have a observe the proof for and in competition to their worry-based ideals.

Section 12: Case Studies: Transforming Perfectionism

In this phase, we present case studies of people who effectively transformed their perfectionist dispositions using the cognitive techniques cited:

Chapter 6: Perfectionism Throughout The Lifespan

Perfectionism is a complex mental trait that could take area in any other way at some stage in numerous life stages. Understanding how perfectionism evolves from youngsters to maturity and spotting its influences at precise elements in life is vital for powerful intervention and assist. This economic disaster delves into the methods perfectionism presents itself at specific a long term and offers strategies for coping and fostering more healthful attitudes.

Section 1: Perfectionism in Childhood

In youth, perfectionism often arises as a response to out of doors expectations and parental impacts. Children may also moreover experience pressure to excel academically, athletically, or artistically, main to the improvement of perfectionist tendencies. Parents who region immoderate emphasis on success or set unrealistically immoderate necessities inadvertently contribute to the emergence of perfectionism Early signs and symptoms and signs of perfectionism embody a worry of making mistakes, seeking out regular approval, and heightened tension related to average overall performance.

Case Study: Emily, a ten-year-antique, avoids trying new sports due to the fear of failure. Her parents' excessive expectancies for her academic normal basic performance have delivered about her perfectionistic mind-set, causing pressure and social isolation.

Section 2: Adolescence and Young Adulthood

During kids and more youthful adulthood, perfectionism can accentuate due to expanded social pressures and the selection for peer validation. The need to fit in, coupled with educational desires and the pursuit of profession goals, can motive heightened perfectionist inclinations. Young adults may additionally enjoy burnout, anxiety, and melancholy due to putting unrealistic requirements for themselves.

Case Study: Alex, an 18-one year-vintage, reviews overwhelming strain and insomnia as he strives to fulfill the expectations of his mother and father, instructors, and buddies. His perfectionism is affecting his intellectual and bodily health.

Section 3: Middle Adulthood

In center adulthood, perfectionism can seem as an excessive want for manipulate over numerous factors of lifestyles, collectively with career, relationships, and look. The fear of failure may additionally lead individuals to keep away from new challenges or take fewer dangers. The pursuit of perfection in profession and own family roles can result in neglecting self-care and personal fulfillment.

Case Study: Sarah, a 40-yr-antique, reveals herself continuously overwhelmed through the desires of her managerial function. She struggles with delegating obligations and on the lookout for assist, fearing that others may not meet her excessive necessities.

Section 4: Later Life

In later lifestyles, perfectionism can take on a super form, driven with the aid of the choice for legacy and leaving an extended lasting effect. The worry of having older and dwindled talents might also moreover make contributions to a heightened need for manage and a choice to provide a perfect image to others. Coping with perfectionism in later life includes embracing the inevitability of exchange and spotting the cost of imperfections.

Case Study: Robert, a retired sixty five-365 days-antique, struggles with accepting his boundaries and is predicated closely on workout routines. He fears acting inclined inside the the front of his person children and resists in search of assist with each day obligations.

Strategies for Coping and Intervention

Psychoeducation: Educate human beings and households approximately the precise manifestations of perfectionism at every life diploma. Raise attention about the terrible results of immoderate perfectionism and its effect on highbrow fitness.

Cognitive Restructuring: Teach human beings to mission perfectionistic thoughts and ideals thru cognitive-behavioral techniques. Help them understand cognitive distortions and update them with more balanced and sensible perspectives.

Mindfulness and Self-Compassion: Encourage the exercising of mindfulness and self-compassion to domesticate a more accepting mind-set towards oneself. Teach individuals to deal with themselves with kindness and data, especially within the face of mistakes or setbacks.

Setting Realistic Goals: Assist humans in placing potential and bendy desires that promote non-public boom with out the stress of perfection. Encourage a focal point on improvement in region of perfection.

Stress Management: Provide strain manipulate techniques, which include relaxation wearing sports activities, deep breathing, and time control strategies. Help people increase healthy coping mechanisms for dealing with perfectionist-related stress.

Seeking Social Support: Encourage individuals to are looking for assist from friends, circle of relatives, or help organizations. Create a secure region for discussing perfectionism-associated stressful situations and sharing reviews.

Therapeutic Intervention: In times of severe perfectionism that intrude with every day functioning, go through in thoughts remedy, together with cognitive-behavioral remedy (CBT) or beauty and determination remedy (ACT). Tailor interventions to the person's precise existence stage and annoying situations.

Section 5: Parental and Societal Influences

Perfectionism frequently takes root in childhood because of a aggregate of parental and societal affects. Parents who excessively emphasize success and region excessive expectancies on their children inadvertently make a contribution to the improvement of perfectionist dispositions. The strain to conform to societal ideals of fulfillment, splendor, and accomplishment can exacerbate those tendencies, leading people to internalize unrealistic necessities.

Case Study: Mia, a 13-one year-vintage, continuously compares herself to the pix of "nice" influencers on social media, primary to feelings of inadequacy and a continuing pursuit of an inconceivable excellent.

Section 6: Coping Mechanisms and Interventions

Addressing perfectionism at amazing life stages calls for tailored interventions and coping strategies:

Childhood: Encourage dad and mom to create a nurturing surroundings that values effort over very last consequences. Teach youngsters that errors are opportunities for increase and analyzing.

Adolescence and Young Adulthood: Emphasize the significance of stability and self-care. Provide tools for putting barriers, dealing with time efficiently, and recognizing the signs and symptoms and signs of burnout.

Middle Adulthood: Help people re-compare priorities and make bigger a revel in of self-worth impartial of out of doors achievements. Foster self-compassion and task the notion that perfection is important for popularity.

Later Life: Support people in embracing the idea of "pinnacle enough" and finding which means that that in imperfection. Guide them in developing a legacy based totally on real values and connections.

Section 7: Cultivating Resilience and Adaptability

While perfectionism may be deeply ingrained, it's miles viable to expand resilience and adaptability:

Flexibility: Encourage human beings to include exchange and unpredictability. Shift the point of interest from rigid control to adaptability and a willingness to navigate demanding situations.

Embracing Failure: Teach that failure is a natural part of lifestyles and an possibility for increase. Help human beings examine from setbacks in desire to seeing them as reflections of their self confidence.

Positive Self-Image: Guide human beings to enlarge a balanced self-picture that recognizes strengths and weaknesses. Encourage them to internalize first-rate affirmations and counteract self-grievance.

Pleasure in Process: Shift the emphasis from outcome to the entertainment of the manner itself. Encourage people to have interaction in sports for the sheer pleasure they devise, in desire to pursuing perfection.

Section eight: Moving Towards Balance

Ultimately, the purpose isn't to put off perfectionism truely but to discover a wholesome stability. Recognize that perfectionism may also moreover in no way simply vanish, however with the proper techniques, it may be controlled effectively:

Continuous Self-Reflection: Encourage normal self-reflected photograph to expose perfectionistic tendencies and their effect. This introspection permits for course correction and model as lifestyles stages trade.

Support Networks: Foster a revel in of network by using connecting people with comparable reports. Support groups can offer validation, understanding, and sensible coping strategies.

Professional Help: In times in which perfectionism critically influences highbrow fitness and each day functioning, suggest in search of assist from intellectual fitness experts. Therapy can offer a steady area for exploring underlying motives and developing customized coping mechanisms.

Section nine: Case Studies in Successful Transformation

Examining real-existence case studies of people who have correctly transformed their perfectionistic tendencies can offer idea and steering:

Childhood: Mark, as quickly as an demanding student scared of making mistakes, learns to embody traumatic conditions and popularity at the delight of analyzing. With the assist of his parents and teachers, he shifts his perspective from looking for out of doors validation to valuing his personal increase.

Adolescence and Young Adulthood: Maya, pressured with the resource of the need to excel in lecturers, extracurricular sports, and social life, reaches a breaking factor. Through remedy, she learns to set sensible goals, prioritize self-care, and appreciate her achievements without overextending herself.

Middle Adulthood: David, a perfectionist government, confronts his worry of failure and delegation. With education, he discovers that his management is strengthened even as he lets in his team individuals to make a contribution their abilities and statistics.

Later Life: Elizabeth, dealing with retirement and the traumatic conditions of growing antique, redefines her self-worth beyond societal beliefs. Through self-compassion and appealing in new pastimes, she finds satisfaction in embracing her imperfections.

Section 10: Exercises for Transformation

Provide practical physical sports for readers to have interaction with as they paintings to transform their perfectionist inclinations:

Journaling Prompts: Encourage readers to mirror on their perfectionist behaviors and their origins. Prompt them to discover the impact of those dispositions on their mental and emotional well-being.

Creating a "Good Enough" List: Guide readers in identifying regions in their lives wherein they are able to encompass the "proper sufficient" desired. This list serves as a reminder to undertaking perfectionism and exercising self-compassion.

Mindfulness Practices: Offer mindfulness sporting activities that assist individuals live gift, famend their emotions, and reduce the tendency to ruminate on perfectionist mind.

Affirmation Development: Assist readers in crafting exceptional affirmations that counteract self-criticism and foster self-elegance. Encourage them to combine the ones affirmations into their every day physical activities.

Section eleven: Navigating Perfectionism in Different Contexts

Examine how perfectionism manifests in various contexts, which incorporates relationships, artwork, and private tasks:

Relationships: Discuss how perfectionism impacts interpersonal dynamics and verbal exchange. Provide techniques for dealing with unrealistic expectancies and selling open speak with loved ones.

Workplace: Explore the impact of perfectionism on activity delight, productivity, and artwork-existence balance. Offer hints for putting limitations, trying to find superb feedback, and managing the fear of failure.

Creative Pursuits: Address the traumatic situations artists, writers, and creators face because of perfectionist inclinations. Guide people in overcoming current blocks and embracing experimentation.

Chapter 7: Creative Expression And Perfectionism

Perfectionism may be a big obstacle to progressive expression and innovative pastimes, because it regularly outcomes in self-grievance, worry of failure, and revolutionary blocks. In this chapter, we will delve into the complicated dating among perfectionism and creativity, exploring the demanding conditions it poses and the strategies that can help humans embody their modern functionality.

Section 1: Perfectionism's Impact on Creativity

Understanding the Creative Process and Perfectionism

Creative expression consists of experimentation, vulnerability, and the willingness to discover new thoughts. However, perfectionism has a dishonest to stifle these factors with the aid of the usage of enforcing rigid requirements and the concern of no longer meeting them. This phase will highlight how perfectionist tendencies can inhibit the modern method and creativity's critical characteristics.

Fear of Imperfection and Self-Censorship

Perfectionism frequently manifests as the worry of manufacturing something that falls quick of 1's immoderate necessities. This fear can result in self-censorship, in which individuals avoid taking dangers or expressing themselves authentically. We'll talk how this fear impacts modern output and prevents artists from exploring new avenues.

Section 2: Overcoming Creative Blocks

Recognizing Perfectionist Thought Patterns

Creative blocks are often rooted in awful concept patterns perpetuated by perfectionism. This section will find out commonplace cognitive distortions, collectively with all-or-not anything questioning and catastrophic predictions, which avoid the innovative manner. By spotting the ones styles, individuals can mission them and cultivate a extra open thoughts-set.

Embracing Mistakes and Imperfections

The worry of creating mistakes can paralyze innovative humans. This segment will emphasize the charge of embracing errors and imperfections as vital factors of the progressive adventure. It will offer practical physical sports to assist artists reframe their thoughts-set on mistakes and use them as getting to know opportunities.

Section 3: Navigating Perfectionism in Creative Fields

Balancing Excellence and Exploration

Striving for excellence isn't always like striving for perfection. This segment will discover the distinction the various and provide steering on locating a balance that permits artists to excel in their craft at the equal time as preserving the liberty to find out new thoughts without the burden of unrealistic standards.

Fostering a Supportive Creative Environment

Perfectionism can thrive in isolation. This phase will communicate the significance of a supportive innovative environment, together with first-class comments, collaboration, and a enjoy of network. It will even cope with the effect of evaluation and competition on perfectionist tendencies.

Section 4: Embracing Imperfection as Catalyst for Innovation

The Role of Imperfection in Innovation

Innovation often arises from embracing imperfections and difficult the popularity quo. This phase will illustrate how imperfections can result in precise and surprising creative effects. Case studies of well-known artists and thinkers who embraced imperfection will spotlight the transformative power of this attitude shift.

Cultivating a Growth Mindset

A growth thoughts-set consists of viewing annoying situations as possibilities for boom and learning. This section will discover how adopting a boom mind-set can counteract perfectionism and promote a willingness to check, adapt, and evolve creatively.

Section 5: Practical Strategies for Creative Expression

Mindfulness and Presence in Creativity

Practicing mindfulness can assist artists live present within the cutting-edge approach, lowering the overpowering recognition on outcomes. This phase will introduce mindfulness techniques that inspire artists to engage in reality with their work and detach from perfectionist expectancies.

Setting Realistic Goals

Setting possible desires is important to counteract perfectionism. This segment will offer guidance on setting precise, measurable, and potential desires that inspire improvement in place of fixating on an improbable give up end result.

Creative Exercises for Embracing Imperfection

This segment will provide a whole lot of modern bodily video games designed to project perfectionist dispositions and inspire playful exploration. These wearing activities can consist of using unconventional substances, embracing "mistakes," and intentionally growing imperfect works of paintings.

Section 6: Fostering Resilience and Self-Compassion in Creativity

Building Resilience

Perfectionism often results in frustration and discouragement at the same time as progressive endeavors do no longer meet impossibly high standards. This section will talk how constructing resilience can assist artists get higher from setbacks, rejections, and moments of self-doubt, letting them preserve pursuing their present day passions.

Practicing Self-Compassion

Self-compassion entails treating oneself with the same kindness and knowledge that one may additionally provide to a near buddy. This segment will emphasize the importance of self-compassion in counteracting the self-crucial inclinations of perfectionism. Practical sports activities will manual artists in cultivating self-compassion as a tool for nurturing their progressive spirit.

Section 7: Creative Vulnerability and Authenticity

Embracing Vulnerability

Creative expression frequently requires vulnerability and the willingness to percentage one's inner thoughts and emotions. This segment will discover how perfectionism can reason self-protecting behaviors that stop actual self-expression. It will offer insights into embracing vulnerability as a supply of power and reference to the target market.

Cultivating Authenticity

Perfectionism can lead artists to offer paintings that is polished however lacks authenticity. This phase will guide people in reconnecting with their proper creative voice and expressing their precise perspective. It will emphasize the cost of imperfections in conveying authenticity and relatability to the intention market.

Section eight: Navigating Feedback and Criticism

Receiving Constructive Feedback

Perfectionism need to make it hard to accumulate feedback with out feeling in my opinion attacked. This phase will provide techniques for artists to method remarks with an open thoughts, spotting it as an possibility for growth in vicinity of a mirrored image in their self confidence.

Overcoming the Fear of Criticism

The worry of complaint can paralyze modern people and save you them from sharing their artwork. This segment will deal with the psychological roots of this fear and provide techniques to little by little triumph over it. It will empower artists to proportion their creations with any luck, even inside the face of functionality critique.

Section 9: Long-Term Growth and Sustainable Creativity

Evolving Creatively

Perfectionism can bring about creative stagnation as artists grow to be trapped in a cycle of producing artwork that meets inflexible requirements. This phase will communicate the significance of evolving creatively, embracing change, and continuously pushing imaginitive barriers for lengthy-term boom and innovation.

Sustainable Creativity

Perfectionism regularly outcomes in burnout and modern fatigue. This phase will discover how adopting a sustainable technique to creativity consists of pacing oneself, placing healthy limitations, and prioritizing self-care. It will offer guidelines for keeping a lifelong innovative exercise without sacrificing well-being.

Section 10: Case Studies and Real-Life Examples

Exploring Artists' Journeys

This section will characteristic case studies and real-lifestyles examples of artists who've grappled with perfectionism and located strategies to triumph over its worrying situations. These reminiscences will provide notion and insights into the numerous paths humans can take to encompass imperfection and foster creativity.

Chapter 8: Breaking Free From Perfectionism

In this bankruptcy, we delve into the technique of breaking unfastened from the grips of perfectionism. We find out sensible steps, strategies, and strategies that people can use to overcome the bad effect of perfectionism on their highbrow well-being and popular nice of life.

Step 1: Recognizing the Perfectionist Patterns

The first step is self-focus. Recognizing perfectionist dispositions and acknowledging their detrimental effects is crucial. This consists of figuring out terrible idea patterns, unrealistic expectations, and the anxiety that perfectionism brings.

Step 2: Challenge Negative Self-Talk

Perfectionism regularly stems from harsh self-criticism and negative self-communicate. This step includes learning to discover and mission these awful mind Cognitive-behavioral techniques may be used to reframe the ones thoughts, replacing them with greater balanced and compassionate self-perceptions.

Step 3: Embracing Self-Compassion

Practicing self-compassion is important in stopping perfectionism. Individuals discover ways to cope with themselves with the same kindness and records they might offer to a chum. This consists of acknowledging errors without self-judgment and embracing imperfections as part of the human experience.

Step four: Setting Realistic Goals

Perfectionists often set improbable desires, leading to continual stress and burnout. Learning to set practical and workable desires is crucial. This step encourages people to interest on improvement in preference to disturbing best results.

Step five: Rethinking Fear of Failure

Addressing the concern of failure is a key thing of overcoming perfectionism.

Individuals discover the idea motives of this fear and enlarge a more wholesome mind-set on errors. They come to recognize that setbacks are opportunities for boom and mastering.

Step 6: Cultivating Mindfulness

Mindfulness strategies help human beings live gift and non-judgmental. Mindfulness allows them to study their mind and emotions with out attaching excessive significance to them. This exercise helps lessen tension and prevents overthinking.

Step 7: Seeking Support

Seeking professional assistance is essential for people suffering with excessive perfectionism. Therapists, counselors, or guide agencies can offer steerage and coping techniques tailor-made to the character's dreams.

Step 8: Gradual Exposure to Imperfection

Engaging in sports sports wherein imperfection is ordinary and even celebrated can assist human beings desensitize themselves to the concern of no longer being best. Creative sports, sports activities, or pastimes wherein development is greater critical than perfect results may be useful.

Step 9: Focus on Self-Value

Shifting the focus from outside validation to internal self-worth is a pivotal step. Individuals work on building their shallowness primarily based completely totally on their inherent charge as humans, instead of their achievements or perfection.

Step 10: Practicing Resilience

Resilience is the capability to get better from setbacks. Learning to deal with disasters and setbacks in a healthy manner is a important ability in overcoming perfectionism. This consists of reframing screw ups as possibilities for increase and development.

Step 11: Celebrating Progress

Perfectionists frequently overlook approximately approximately to have an awesome time their achievements because of the fact they will be fixated on what went wrong. This step consists of acknowledging and celebrating each small step and fulfillment, reinforcing the concept that development is good sized and precious.

ztep 12: Embracing Imperfection as Strength

The final step is embracing imperfection as a deliver of power and authenticity. Individuals have a examine that their imperfections motive them to particular and relatable. Embracing imperfection allows foster creativity, innovation, and significant connections with others.

Step 13: Building a Supportive Environment

Creating a supportive environment is critical for preserving improvement. This involves surrounding oneself with folks that respect and inspire authenticity, in vicinity of perfection. Cultivating connections with people who price private boom and nicely-being allows improve the journey a long way from perfectionism.

Step 14: Practicing Vulnerability

Perfectionism often stems from a fear of being inclined and exposing one's flaws. Practicing vulnerability approach sharing one's worrying conditions and imperfections with trusted human beings. This not handiest fosters real connections but additionally reduces the isolation that perfectionism can convey.

Step 15: Reshaping the Definition of Success

Perfectionists frequently tie their self-worth to external achievements. This step includes redefining fulfillment in terms of private boom, fulfillment, and the extraordinary impact one has on others. Shifting the point of interest far from external validation reduces the strain to be ideal.

Step 16: Cultivating Patience

Overcoming perfectionism is a slow manner. Cultivating staying electricity is critical due to the truth exchange takes time. Individuals discover ways to be affected individual with themselves as they navigate setbacks, unlearn antique behavior, and undertake new techniques of thinking and behaving.

Step 17: Challenging All-or-Nothing Thinking

Perfectionists have a propensity to count on in black-and-white phrases – something is each best or a failure. Challenging this all-or-now not some factor thinking consists of recognizing the grey regions. Accepting that excellence can coexist with imperfection allows for a greater balanced and realistic attitude.

Step 18: Redirecting Perfectionist Energy

Perfectionists frequently private a robust art work ethic and interest to element. Redirecting those trends inside the direction of advantageous pastimes, in area of perfection-looking for, may be empowering.

Focusing on projects and obligations that align with private values fosters a enjoy of reason and pride.

Step 19: Practicing Gratitude

Cultivating gratitude shifts the focus from what is missing to what is already gift. By acknowledging the positives in existence, people counteract the tendency to obsess over shortcomings. This exercise enhances typical well-being and minimizes perfectionist tendencies.

Step 20: Celebrating Mistakes as Learning Opportunities

Viewing mistakes as stepping stones to growth is a transformative attitude. Individuals study to research errors, extract treasured training, and combine them into future endeavors. Embracing this thoughts-set reduces the concern of failure and encourages taking calculated risks.

Step 21: Engaging in Self-Reflection

Regular self-mirrored photograph allows humans to song their improvement, select out out triggers, and test out the effectiveness of their techniques. Journaling, meditation, or in truth setting apart time for introspection permits keep recognition and enables ongoing private development.

Step 22: Acknowledging the Journey

Perfectionism can be deeply ingrained and breaking loose from it's miles a large accomplishment. Acknowledging the development made, no matter how small, reinforces a experience of success and motivation to keep on the adventure of self-discovery and boom.

Step 23: Embracing the Unpredictable

Perfectionism thrives on predictability and control. Embracing the unpredictable nature of lifestyles lets in human beings to conform to adjustments, get hold of uncertainties, and discover splendor within the unexpected. This shift in mind-set promotes resilience and decreases tension.

Step 24: Sharing the Journey

As people make development in overcoming perfectionism, sharing their testimonies with others may be inspiring and impactful. By sharing private memories, insights, and techniques, they make a contribution to a way of life of openness and self-popularity, encouraging others to embark on comparable trips.

Chapter 9: Embracing Imperfection

In this very last financial smash, we delve into the transformative adventure of embracing imperfection and the way it outcomes in private increase, resilience, and a more fulfilled existence. We'll discover the idea of imperfection as a catalyst for terrific trade and offer practical techniques to shift some distance from the grip of perfectionism.

Section 1: The Beauty of Imperfection

In the hole section, we spotlight the ambiguity of imperfection how it could be each liberating and provoking. We talk how the pursuit of perfection regularly leaves us feeling unfulfilled and trapped in a cycle of in no way-completing wishes. By comparison, embracing imperfection permits us to enjoy the pleasure of authenticity and freedom from unrealistic expectations. Real-existence examples and anecdotes illustrate how human beings have flourished via accepting their imperfections.

Section 2: The Role of Imperfection in Personal Growth

This segment explores how imperfections feature stepping stones to private growth. We talk how demanding situations and screw ups provide valuable commands that shape our man or woman and resilience. We delve into the concept of a boom thoughts-set, highlighting how viewing setbacks as opportunities for gaining knowledge of can reason extra self-discovery and improvement. We gift studies that display how folks that consist of their imperfections normally have a propensity to boom extra emotional intelligence and versatility.

Section 3: Cultivating Resilience thru Imperfection

Building on the concept of personal boom, we study how imperfections contribute to resilience. We find out how handling adversity and overcoming limitations can bring together inner power and the capability to get higher from setbacks. Through real-global testimonies and studies, we illustrate how humans who have embraced imperfection are better equipped to navigate existence's worrying conditions with grace and resolution.

Section 4: Practical Strategies for Embracing Imperfection

This section offers a toolkit of realistic techniques for readers to start embracing imperfection of their lives. We provide step-through-step guidance on a way to shift from a perfectionist mind-set to one that values development and authenticity:

1. Mindfulness Practices:We introduce mindfulness techniques that help people become privy to their perfectionist tendencies and terrible concept patterns. By staying present and non-judgmental, readers can begin dismantling the automatic drive for flawlessness.

2. Self-Compassion: We delve into the concept of self-compassion and deliver an

cause of how treating oneself with kindness and facts can counteract the tough self-grievance that regularly accompanies perfectionism. We provide bodily activities to domesticate self-compassion and self-love.

three. Setting Realistic Goals: We manual readers in setting ability and meaningful desires that target non-public increase in location of ideal consequences. Strategies for breaking down massive dreams into manageable steps are explored.

4. Learning from Mistakes: We emphasize the importance of embracing errors and screw ups as possibilities for increase. By reframing errors as learning reports, readers can shift their mindset and reduce the worry of failure.

5. Letting Go of Comparisons: We communicate the dangerous nature of constant evaluation to others and provide strategies to increase a extra balanced self-assessment technique. Celebrating man or woman improvement and distinctiveness turns into a cornerstone of this exercise.

Section 5: Sustaining a Life Beyond Perfection

In the concluding segment, we spotlight the lasting effect of embracing imperfection. We address the functionality traumatic situations readers might also stumble upon on their journey and provide recommendation for keeping a existence that values improvement, authenticity, and self-compassion:

Building a Support Network: We emphasize the significance of surrounding oneself with supportive folks that recognize the journey closer to embracing imperfection.

Regular Reflection:We inspire readers to have interaction in ordinary self-mirrored photograph to track their progress and select out areas in which perfectionist dispositions might likely resurface.

Continual Growth: We stress that embracing imperfection is an ongoing manner. Just as non-public increase is non-prevent, so is the paintings of transferring past perfectionism.

We offer motivation and strategies to maintain a willpower to this change.

Section 6: Applying Imperfection to Different Aspects of Life

Expanding on the sensible strategies cited earlier, this segment explores how embracing imperfection can truely impact numerous areas of existence:

Work and Career: We take a look at how transferring from perfectionism to a focus on development can bring about multiplied undertaking pleasure, creativity, and innovation. Readers discover ways to set realistic expectancies for themselves and manipulate art work-associated pressure extra successfully.

Relationships: We delve into how embracing imperfection can decorate private relationships. By letting pass of unrealistic expectations, people can foster deeper connections, powerful conversation, and empathy internal their relationships.

Parenting and Education:We communicate the significance of selling a boom-oriented mindset in children, encouraging them to have a look at from disasters and setbacks. Parents and educators benefit insights into nurturing resilience and self-splendor in young minds.

Physical and Mental Health:We emphasize the relationship among perfectionism and mental fitness issues collectively with anxiety and despair. Practical strategies are supplied for cultivating self-care practices, self-compassion, and a wholesome self-picture.

Section 7: Stories of Transformation

In this inspiring phase, we percentage stories of humans who have effectively transformed their lives through embracing imperfection. Through firsthand bills and interviews, readers advantage insights into the annoying situations confronted, the techniques done, and the profound changes experienced. These recollections function beacons of desire and motivation for readers embarking on their very own journeys toward embracing imperfection.

Section eight: Overcoming Resistance and Staying the Course

Acknowledging that the path to embracing imperfection isn't always with out its boundaries, this section addresses not unusual disturbing situations and offers strategies for overcoming resistance:

Fear of Vulnerability: We explore the priority of being judged or rejected even as revealing one's imperfections. Practical sports sports help readers assemble the courage to be inclined and real.

Reverting to Perfectionism:We talk how antique conduct die hard and offer techniques to understand and counteract moments while the pull of perfectionism returns.

Coping with External Pressures:We guide readers at the manner to deal with societal pressures and expectations that often improve the force for perfection. Strategies for putting boundaries and placing forward one's private values are presented.

Section 9: The Ongoing Journey

In this final section, we emphasize that embracing imperfection isn't always a holiday spot however an ongoing journey. We reiterate the importance of self-compassion, resilience, and continuous growth:

Self-Celebration: We encourage readers to frequently have a very good time their development and acknowledge the strides they've made in letting pass of perfectionism.

Mindful Living: We discover how mindfulness practices can help people stay attuned to their thoughts and behaviors, making it less difficult to trap perfectionist dispositions in advance than they take maintain.

Community and Support: We emphasize the price of community and recommend attempting to find ongoing assist from pals, circle of relatives, or useful resource agencies that apprehend the journey.

Section 10: The Ripple Effect of Embracing Imperfection

In this section, we delve into how embracing imperfection could have a first rate ripple impact on society, relationships, and beyond:

Social Impact: We communicate how folks that allow bypass of perfectionism frequently inspire those spherical them to do the identical. By modeling self-recognition and authenticity, they make contributions to a cultural shift away from unrealistic standards.

Leadership and Empowerment: We discover how leaders who encompass imperfection can create greater healthy paintings environments, foster innovation, and empower their agencies. Authentic leaders are greater relatable, approachable, and effective.

Chapter 10: A Brief Introduction To Perfectionism

Perfectionism is a complex character trait and cognitive sample characterized through the maintenance of unrealistically high requirements for oneself or others and the unrelenting pursuit of excellence at any rate. It can take much office work, every with its private set of signs and symptoms and signs and symptoms and functionality outcomes on a person's health and relationships.

Individualistic idealisation is based totally on one's personal set of standards for achievement. People who are perfectionists of their very very very own eyes are frequently harsh critics of them and are driven by using manner of an excessive need to degree as a good buy as their very own multiplied necessities. They have to enjoy they want to attempt for perfection, looking for approval from others through their successes. While this form of perfectionism can in reality yield a few remarkable consequences, it isn't always without its emotional prices, as its practitioners frequently be anxious through self-doubt, dread of failure, and an normal feeling of in no way being proper sufficient.

External influences and cultural expectancies offer rise to socially imposed perfectionism. Those who be afflicted by socially mandated perfectionism feel compelled to perform as an awful lot as the expectancies of their circle of relatives, buddies, and society at huge. This kind of perfectionism is specially unstable because it makes humans revel in trapped and relying on others' recognition and praise. Anxiety, melancholy, and a lack of touch with one's actual self can give up result from a consistent preoccupation with captivating others and a fear of grievance.

Having high necessities for the people around you is an example of "one-of-a-type-oriented perfectionism. Relationships can end up strained whilst one man or woman is continuously striving for perfection, that could cause others feeling green with envy and faraway. As a result in their preoccupation with the failings they recognize in others, humans who be bothered by means of "other-orientated perfectionism" can also have problem accepting and assisting others for who they simply are.

It is crucial to understand that perfectionism is not always a awful thing. When stored in test, it can feature an notion for improvement and achievement. When perfectionism will become immoderate and all-consuming, however, it is able to have excessive horrible outcomes on one's emotional well-being, interpersonal connections, and fashionable tremendous of life.

Individual character tendencies, upbringing, cultural affects, and society conventions can all play a function in shaping someone's diploma of perfectionism. Understanding the results of perfectionism and its root motives calls for first identifying the various manifestations of the trait. Management and mitigation of perfectionism's harmful impacts can also need encouragement of self-compassion, promoting of a boom mindset, and session with intellectual health professionals. A happier and greater efficient life can be the end result of a well-rounded technique that consists of every reason-putting and popularity of human fallibility.

Accepting one's humanity and striving for a more well-rounded lifestyles aren't at the identical time precise. It entails accepting oneself and others at the same time as having flaws. The secret's to look failure and setbacks for what they in reality are: possibilities to observe and increase.

One of the most crucial subjects you could do to free your self from perfectionism is to schooling self-compassion. The overwhelming pressure to be outstanding may be decreased through manner of treating oneself kindly, accepting that errors are inevitable, and showing oneself the equal care and know-how one suggests to others.

The development of a increase thoughts-set, along with self-compassion, may additionally have profound outcomes. Adopting a growth mind-set includes reinterpreting setbacks and errors as studying reminiscences in location of private reflections approximately competence. When human beings make this highbrow alternate, they may be capable of view obstacles now not as insurmountable but as stepping stones on the path to success.

Those who conflict with perfectionism also can additionally advantage from talking therapy or counselling. You can studies more approximately the origins of perfectionism and the way to address its results through consulting a intellectual health professional. A therapist can assist a customer triumph over their perfectionism and benefit a more balanced view in their personal successes and setbacks.

The continuation of perfectionism may be hindered with the aid of encouraging a way of lifestyles that values strive, improvement, and resilience over perfect effects. Contributing to a more wholesome and greater compassionate society may be as smooth as encouraging human beings to realize and look at from their errors, encouraging artwork-lifestyles stability, and opposing the belief of steady evaluation with others.

It's beneficial to maintain in thoughts that perfectionism isn't black-and-white, and that high-quality human beings will display diverse degrees of the trait in distinct contexts. Better interactions and relationships can give up stop result from an prolonged capacity for self- and other-cognizance that sample popularity fosters.

The purpose of the direction far from perfectionism is not perfection a lot as it is the recognition of the splendor that includes being human, flaws and all. Adopting a boom mind-set and studying to encompass our flaws has been verified to boom resiliency and happiness inside the face of adversity.

Accepting one's flaws and giving up on the proper are not similar to settling for 2d great or giving up on one's dreams in life. Instead, it permits for extra right and pleasing strategies to improve in a single's profession and personal lifestyles.

The remedy of anxiety and anxiety is one of the finest blessings of forsaking perfectionism. When people forestall trying so hard to be fine, they find out a stunning amount of liberation. They won't need to worry a lot about the very last product and can as an possibility commit themselves to the method of gaining knowledge of and boom.

Adopting a boom mind-set and mastering to embody our flaws strengthens our capacity to bounce back from adversity. They recognize that setbacks are not personal indictments, however as a substitute activities to extend and enhance. Because of their resilience, they are capable of get over setbacks and cross ahead with renewed strength and clear up.

Moreover, letting up of perfectionism can bring about deeper, extra actual connections with one-of-a-kind human beings. Vulnerability and the admission of flaws permit human beings to connect with others on a deeper diploma. By letting their guard down, humans are able to have deeper, extra large connections with every different, which in turn allows them weather life's inevitable storms.

In the industrial company worldwide, letting cross of the want for perfection may be a catalyst for ultra-modern mind and processes. When human beings undertake a more adaptable mind-set, they may be extra able to take a look at with new ideas, anticipate creatively, and take little dangers. If you're willing to strive new topics, you could give you modern thoughts that would not have been feasible in case you had been striving for perfection.

Many people record feeling happier and additional fulfilled because of having decreased their requirements for achievement. When successes are celebrated, they function idea in desire to distraction from the following seemingly insurmountable purpose. A more positive and properly-rounded outlook on existence is viable after making this transition.

The influences of life-style, upbringing, and individual records on your quest for perfection

One's upbringing forms their idea of perfection at a formative age. It is viable for youngsters to internalize the belief that some detail an lousy lot less than perfection is unacceptable if they may be nurtured in a culture that locations an excessive emphasis on success and immoderate achievements. It can be tough for children to just accept imperfection as a normal a part of the analyzing and development device whilst well-that means dad and mom, trying to encourage them, promote an unshakable notion that errors are disasters.

One's personal life reviews could have a function within the maturation of perfectionist tendencies. After experiencing trauma or extraordinary disappointments, some humans want to exert manage over their lives via perfectionism. As an try to cope with the turmoil and uncertainty of life, striving for perfection can provide a feel of order and stability.

Individuals may additionally furthermore vicinity unreasonable goals on themselves in their quest for perfection. These beliefs are not feasible to achieve, and as a end result, they result in a in no manner-completing spiral of self-doubt and complaint. Long-term exposure to this shape of pressure can cause emotional and intellectual breakdowns.

Social media and the subculture of assessment they foster have made perfectionism dispositions more good sized. People might also moreover moreover enjoy unworthy and compelled to stay as much as not possible beliefs if they'll be constantly bombarded with carefully produced photographs of "perfect" lives and "ideal" our our our bodies.

The pursuit of perfection also can come to be entangled with massive societal norms and customs. The electricity for perfection may be seen as a sign of area and ambition in a few societies, at the same time as in others it is able to be associated with a fear of complaint and embarrassment.

Some ought to argue that perfectionists are the ones who push society ahead and create new mind, notwithstanding the drawbacks. While this will be real to a sure quantity, there are commonly extra negative effects associated with striving for perfection than nice ones.

In order to encourage a more healthy and more balanced manner of existence, it's far essential to understand and cope with the motives of perfectionism. In order to interrupt loose from perfectionism, it could be useful to education self-compassion, accept vulnerability, and charge attempt over results. Individuals can sense favored for who they're as human beings, in vicinity of for what they've got completed, at the identical time as human beings undertaking society necessities and advocate for a extra compassionate and tolerant subculture.

Individuals may additionally advantage a sense of liberation and genuineness with the aid of accepting their flaws. They can loose themselves from the stress to be ideal, establishing up new possibilities for improvement, training, and self-discovery. Accepting setbacks as studying critiques strengthens resilience and improves mind-set on existence.

To conquer perfectionism, it's far important to surround oneself with individuals who will aid and apprehend them. The first step is to encourage candid discussions about highbrow fitness and the problems of aiming for perfection. The veneer of perfection may be damaged and a enjoy of camaraderie installation via the use of encouraging openness and sharing personal disturbing situations.

The price of education in stopping the strain to be amazing can not be overstated. Self-compassion, resilience, and healthy cause-placing are all competencies that could assist humans of any age deal with the inevitable problems they'll face in lifestyles. We might also moreover moreover set them up for an entire life of success and self-apprehend if we teach them to persevere through failure and be for the reason that perfection is each no longer viable and useless.

Those who battle with perfectionism also can discover treatment and counselling to be pretty beneficial. Getting expert assist can permit humans to discover the origins in their perfectionism, heal from emotional wounds, and studies powerful coping strategies so that it will circulate thru lifestyles with more self perception and much less anxiety.

Rethinking the importance of achievement and success as a collective is critical. Reducing the pressure to reach perfection specifically areas of lifestyles can be executed thru expanding the definition of achievement beyond conventional markers and recognising a whole lot of accomplishments.

The dangerous influences of perfectionism may be mitigated with the resource of encouraging a way of life that values gadget above product. The recognition may be shifted from an unrealistic sizable of perfection to a healthy pursuit of private growth and development by using manner of recognising and applauding the fortitude it takes to attempt to have a look at, even within the face of failure.

Reducing the rate positioned on perfectionism within the place of job has been confirmed to enhance morale and productivity. Worker engagement and motivation are better at corporations that care about their personnel' health, career improvement, and remarkable of existence outdoor of labor. Companies can encourage risk-taking and the development of novel methods by using the usage of manner of reminding human beings that innovation frequently calls for a learning curve.

The media and advertising and marketing and advertising and marketing have an obligation to offer greater nuanced and inclusive requirements of fulfillment and splendor to their audiences. Media stores also can assist humans, mainly more youthful humans, have a extra incredible body photograph and revel in of self confidence through manner of keeping off airbrushed and quite excellent photos.

When humans forestall trying so difficult to be terrific, they have got extra highbrow and emotional space to pursue the subjects that genuinely count number to them and make a difference in the international. If this trend keeps, our lifestyle also can eventually end up one wherein human beings are happier, extra connected, and extra empathetic.

The damaging effects of perfectionism on one's psyche and relationships

Those who attempt for perfection normally lay unreasonable expectancies on themselves, which can be next to not possible to hold. Consequently, human beings might also moreover struggle with an ongoing experience of inadequacy and self-doubt, with the belief that they may be now not pinnacle enough being bolstered with each new setback or mistakes. Their highbrow health, and consequently their experience of self-worth and arrogance, can go through due to this regular motion of negative self-communicate.

Striving for perfection can be a stumbling block to growing improvement in existence. Individuals aren't capable of branch out and pursue new opportunities due to the fact they're terrified of making errors or taking dangers. People who strive for perfection will be inclined to keep away from situations wherein they'll no longer proper away thrive, rather than embracing issues and studying from setbacks. Avoiding new demanding situations must make a person stuck of their strategies, lowering their probabilities of enhancing in all regions of lifestyles.

The results of perfectionism in interpersonal relationships may be devastating. Their incessant pursuit of perfection seeps into their relationships with others, raising expectancies that might in no way be met. Those who strive for perfection frequently end up important, judgmental, or emotionally indifferent on the same time as the ones spherical them necessarily fall quick of their lofty ideals. This shape of conduct can energy loved ones away and perpetuate a cycle of unhappiness and resentment, that could in the end cause emotions of loneliness.

The potential to paintings properly with others, each in my view and professionally, additionally can be negatively impacted thru perfectionism. A perfectionist's reluctance to consider others or distribute paintings might possibly stymie employer efforts. The energy to normally be in price should make one inflexible and inflexible, alienating each buddies and coworkers.

The quest for perfection is, in the end, doomed to failure. Demanding perfection from oneself or others is a surefire manner to end up disillusioned and unhappy. Perfectionism can obstruct innovation, fortitude, and versatility, in choice to encouraging development and fulfillment.

It is crucial for better highbrow fitness, developing meaningful relationships, and private improvement to apprehend and deal with perfectionism. To live a happier and extra satisfactory lifestyles, it's far essential to education self-compassion, take delivery of imperfections, and be willing to investigate from mistakes. In order to overcome the detrimental consequences of perfectionism and develop a greater balanced and resilient thoughts-set on life, it is probably useful to seeking out guide from highbrow fitness experts or to interact in self-reflective practises.

Those who are able to break unfastened from the chains of perfectionism often discover that their lives trade dramatically in loads of tactics. Mental and emotional fitness boom whilst one takes a greater centered and being involved stance inside the route in their non-public development and development.

When people decrease their expectations for themselves and lighten up about in no way accomplishing them, they frequently report a dramatic decrease in stress and anxiety. A revel in of self-recognition and self-compassion can flourish at the equal time as one accepts that making mistakes and being fallacious are everyday and expected factors of being human. The exceptional effects on one's intellectual fitness and resilience inside the face of adversity are amplified via adopting this new frame of thoughts.

When it entails developing as a person, letting bypass of perfectionism frees you to take on new memories with energy. When humans triumph over their fear of failure, they will be free to strive new topics and push themselves past their consolation zones. The capability to take grievance in stride and use it to decorate one's overall performance is an indicator of success-oriented humans.

As perfectionism is dropped, human beings may additionally additionally discover they will be greater receptive to grievance and recommendations. They shift their mind-set on complaint and discover ways to use it to make themselves better. Their openness to grievance boosts their ability to select up new information and enhance their average overall performance.

It takes effort and time to conquer perfectionism, and you'll likely enjoy a few disappointment along the way. Still, improvement towards self-recognition and compassion leads to stepped forward health and happiness. Individuals can discover assist in this path to trade through wearing out mindfulness practises, present gadget cognitive-behavioral therapy, or leaning on supportive cherished ones.

The capability to get better from disasters and difficulties improves due to letting pass of perfectionism. The disability to get better from setbacks is a commonplace problem amongst perfectionists thinking about that they've a tendency to internalise bad effects. One's capacity to recover from failure improves once they develop a healthful attitude on failure and discover ways to gather their private humanity. They undertake a growth mind-set, because of this they view setbacks now not as insurmountable barriers however as opportunities for development.

Letting flow of perfectionism also can unharness your internal innovator. People who battle with perfectionism regularly war to be innovative because of the fact they're afraid to attempt new subjects for fear of failing. But while humans supply themselves permission to find out and make errors, they unleash their full creative capability. Taking dangers and questioning established practices are commonplace belongings of innovation.

The difference among wholesome perfectionism and excellence

At first appearance, the pursuit of excellence and an obsessive obsession with perfection also can seem like identical. Both need striving for excellence and a dedication to improving oneself constantly. As we float deeper into their essence, but, we discover key versions that account for his or her specific outcomes and intellectual consequences.

The pursuit of greatness is a healthful and green manner to decorate one's career and oneself. It requires aiming excessive and running tough to gather fulfillment. The emphasis is on growing one's ability, gaining knowledge from past research, and handling adversity head-on with grit and fortitude. Excellence is propelled thru enthusiasm, inquisitiveness, and a honest yearning for improvement. It recognises that no character is right and that the manner itself is big.

However, horrific perfectionism is pushed through feelings of inadequacy and anxiety. Some people, known as perfectionists, revel in an terrific need to keep away from even the arrival of imperfection. They get caught in an limitless loop of self-criticism and evaluating themselves to impossible requirements. Mistakes are seen as private disasters rather as mastering reviews, which perpetuates a cycle of worry and anger.

The pursuit of greatness fosters a attitude this is open and willing to change. It takes under attention the fact that consequences cannot generally be assured and that adjustments may be required. However, horrible perfectionism promotes stress and a fear of failure, which in turn may additionally cause one to avoid taking on new demanding situations.

The impact on human beings's emotions is a similarly distinguishing function. The pursuit of excellence is associated with a more high-quality frame of thoughts, one this is happy with improvement even though it is not perfect. This approach promotes emotional fitness and could increase self assure.

On the flip detail, awful levels of perfectionism can also have negative effects on one's psyche. The stress, despair, and fatigue that would result from feeling such as you want to be best may be devastating. Many perfectionists experience an limitless loop of self-doubt because of their persistent belief that their exceptional efforts are in no way proper sufficient.

There is also a big distinction in the way the ones philosophies have an impact on interpersonal connections. Aiming immoderate and actively searching for comments and enter from others has an inclination to foster a way of life of cooperation, teamwork, and open communicate. On the opportunity hand, pathological perfectionism can stress relationships because individuals who be afflicted via it tend to project their non-public unreasonable necessities onto those spherical them.

Pursuing excellence in one's revolutionary endeavours ends in the improvement of 1's capabilities and the advent of more and more splendid paintings. Pursuing greatness is useful for creators of all stripes because it encourages them to keep developing their know-how. They see their current gadget as an opportunity to find out who they're and the area spherical them.

However, unhealthy perfectionism can stifle innovation. The dread of failure can paralyse artists, stopping them from taking risks and developing their craft. Trying to reap a degree of perfection this is not possible to gain can turn the innovative way right proper into a chore as opposed to a manner of self-expression.

It's crucial to keep in thoughts that some human beings need to vacillate among perfect and awful stages of perfectionism counting on their activities or man or woman tendencies, so it's far critical to draw a smooth line among the 2. Understanding the motivations underlying one's pursuit of immoderate requirements and assessing the impact on one's well-being are every notably aided with the useful resource of a healthy dose of self-recognition.

Chapter 11: The Mind Of The Perfectionist

Perfectionists regularly be troubled through "all-or-not whatever" questioning, a form of cognitive distortion. They have a binary worldview and take into account themselves losers within the event that they're now not nice at a few issue they're attempting. This excessive dualism prevents the development of nuanced views and results in a persistent enjoy of inadequacy.

People who attempt for perfection often have interaction in "catastrophizing," in which they exaggerate the functionality terrible results in their moves. They worry that the smallest slip-up may additionally result in the prevent of the sector on account that they have such excessive requirements for the whole lot. This paralyzing dread of rejection maintains humans from taking probabilities and seizing clean possibilities.

Mind-analyzing is each special cognitive distortion connected to perfectionism, wherein people with this sickness incorrectly count on that other humans look at them in fact as harshly as they do. They continuously fear that others are judging and criticising them due to the fact they trust they're being watched and judged.

Overgeneralization is a lure that many perfectionists fall into; they take complaint or failure in a single area and use it to justify giving up on other additives of their lives. As a result, they'll lose self belief, be a good deal much less possibly to strive new subjects, and be a great deal much less open to reading from their failures.

To add insult to injury, perfectionists regularly use "emotional reasoning," the fallacy that one's emotions as it should be represent the area. For this reason, humans take their non-public perceptions of failure and inadequacy as gospel. The vicious cycle of perfectionism is maintained due to the truth the person's destructive self-belief is reinforced by using way of the use of their very own internal validation of ugly emotions.

Those who strive for perfection may additionally additionally have trouble "discounting the exquisite," a highbrow nation wherein they minimise their very personal achievements through using downplaying their importance or attributing their victories to top fortune in preference to their very own difficult artwork. This leads them to continuously attempt for extra and hold up an impossible fine, which leaves them feeling unfulfilled and unhappy.

Perfectionists are also liable to using "need to" phrases, which set extraordinarily excessive necessities for their very personal performance. They have unrealistic expectations of themselves and are considerably difficult on themselves when they fall brief.

The in no manner-finishing pursuit of perfection is fueled in detail through the aforementioned cognitive illusions. To free oneself from this kind of wondering, it's far necessary to end up aware of one's very very personal unfavourable belief patterns and to replace them with more rational and traumatic ones. Those who strive for perfection may additionally moreover find extra happiness and fitness through reading to consist of imperfection, take shipping of mistakes as a crucial a part of reading, and prioritise increase above perfection.

Moreover, a perfectionist's lifestyles can be extensively altered through manner in their in no manner-completing quest for perfection. They can start prioritising their art work or targets over their buddies, family, and even themselves. Burnout, infection, and strained relationships with loved ones can all end result from a a person placing undue pressure on oneself.

Those who attempt for perfection may additionally furthermore have problem making selections. Fear of making a horrific choice can paralyse people and motive them to miss out on possibilities. Since they worry loads about falling quick of their very personal lofty expectations, they regularly avoid taking up new responsibilities clearly.

These humans are at risk of perfectionism, that could lead them to revel in lonely and remoted. They won't reach out for assist or be open approximately their problems due to the reality they fear others will word how fragile they're. The terrible notion styles and cognitive distortions already found in the ones humans are exacerbated via their solitude.

It's possible that perfectionists have hassle going for walks in companies. They can also additionally have hassle delegating due to the truth they worry no individual else can do a excellent project. Stress, burnout, and interpersonal tensions within the place of work can all upward thrust as a result.

Also, striving for perfection may additionally stifle originality and creativeness. The lack of ability to take opportunities and the avoidance of trying new things are each outcomes of being terrified of making mistakes. Therefore, a perfectionist must stick to traditional strategies and keep away from stretching their abilities by way of using venturing outdoor their consolation region.

It's crucial to undergo in thoughts that the satisfactory intentions within the lower again of perfectionism not often outweigh its negative results. People who strive for perfection frequently have a sturdy power to achieve success. When their obsession with perfection starts offevolved offevolved to negatively impact their intellectual fitness and prevent them from dwelling inside the second, they have got a trouble.

Redefining what constitutes fulfillment can be essential for perfectionists as they learn to education self-compassion and confront their cognitive biases. They can redirect their attention from outdoor successes and conforming to societal norms of perfection to inner improvement, fortitude, and delight.

For perfectionists, developing a improvement mindset might be mainly beneficial. To gain this, one need to take delivery of the truth that capability and competence are malleable and can be cultivated through take a look at and training. An man or woman with a improvement mind-set sees screw ups and problems as gaining knowledge of critiques in place of caution signs of weakness.

It's vital to domesticate a feel of self confidence that is not relying on one's achievements. Perfectionists can lessen their need on outside validation and create a greater steady base for their conceitedness with the aid of gaining knowledge of to recognise and fee their innate without a doubt properly well worth as people, other than their achievements.

Overcoming perfectionism can result in newfound appreciation for self-care and the price of limits. Saying "no" to vain requests and excessive expectancies can free you as a tremendous deal as pursue pursuits that absolutely depend.

It might also moreover help to surround your self with folks who percent your ideals and who are inclined that will help you thru the problems of perfectionism. Having a help network of people who understand what you are going via and have been there themselves may be quite beneficial.

Insecurities and what form of you need the approval of others

People who try to be best typically generally tend to region extraordinarily excessive requirements on their non-public normal normal performance. The preference for perfection typically arises from a crippling tension about making errors. Because they count on perfection in the whole lot they do, even ordinary duties bring forth emotions of anxiety and tension. They begin associating their charge with what they accomplish, and any setback looks as if an attack on who they will be.

Perfectionists look to others for affirmation in their very very own fee. This need for steady outside confirmation of one's capability and truely virtually really worth can come to be an horrible obsession. Getting stated or praised permits them feel better approximately themselves and their capabilities for a hint while. They revel in better for a bit at the same time as, but fast apprehend they want more affirmation to preserve their arrogance up.

The cycle of needing and attempting to find approval from others is destructive. They start to experience inferior because of the reality they need to depend on the approval of others. As a end end result, people may be hesitant to strive new things for fear of being judged negatively inside the occasion that they do no longer prevail. When human beings are too involved about what extraordinary human beings will recollect them, they regularly preserve themselves decrease lower back from undertaking their first-class capability.

In the mind of a perfectionist, the 2 are inextricably related: the worry of failure and the need for external affirmation. When humans are frightened of failing, they often are searching for outdoor confirmation as a coping method. Codependency can impact a person's achievement in university, artwork, relationships, and different regions of lifestyles. Long-term publicity might also result in exhaustion, fear, and a modern feel of not measuring up.

Perfectionists want to learn to embody imperfection and get hold of that failure is a vital a part of development. A more strong and top notch experience of self may be advanced through the exercise of accepting one's flaws and developing from one's disasters. The pursuit of 1's very very own revel in of truly in reality worth and the recognition of one's private increase, no matter the approval of others, can purpose a extra stable and fulfilling existence.

Perfectionists can benefit substantially from self-care regimens and mindfulness wearing sports. Fear of failure is often followed via tension and self-doubt, but running toward mindfulness strategies like meditation or deep breathing can help alleviate the ones feelings. Balance may be restored and the need for ongoing validation decreased if self-care sports activities like pastimes, exercising, and time spent in nature are prioritised.

As human beings discover ways to permit flow into of their want for perfection, they will moreover rediscover their functionality for particular belief and motion. They triumph over their aversion to creating mistakes, which permits them to try new subjects and growth their creativity. If you are caught within the limits of perfectionism, analyzing to embody uncertainty and tolerate ambiguity can also assist you ruin through to new insights and possibilities.

As perfectionists maintain their journey in the course of overcoming their worry of failure and their want for outside validation, they will moreover begin to delve more deeply into the idea of self-compassion. Practising self-compassion is providing your self with the equal empathy and encouragement you'll provide to an top notch pal going through a hard time. It necessitates accepting that flaws and mistakes are an inevitable trouble of being human.

Writing in a journal can assist perfectionists better understand their inner workings. They can efficiently and anonymously paintings through their concerns, worries, and self-doubt via writing in a magazine. Insights obtained thru this approach may be used to better understand the reasons and effects of perfectionism, taking into account greater fruitful introspection and improvement.

Perfectionists may experience instances of vulnerability as they keep on the direction in the direction of letting move of perfectionism. The danger of sadness and rejection that includes displaying emotion may be tough for perfectionists. However, allowing oneself to revel in uncovered can be releasing since it results in more right connections with others and a extra feeling of belonging.

How striving for perfection contributes to emotional distress

The consistent want to enhance and attain an impossible motive may want to make perfectionism a double-edged blade that damages our psyche. The want for absolute perfection may appear to be a commendable characteristic, one that propels us to extra heights. However, this outward self belief commonly conceals a deep-seated dread of rejection and humiliation.

Anxiety follows the perfectionist round like a shadow, following his or her each movement. Worry and apprehension flourish even as there may be a consistent pressure to fulfil unrealistic expectancies. Those who strive for perfection are usually afflicted via the concern that they'll be judged negatively. Worrying approximately what precise humans might imagine amplifies this worry, making even habitual sports sports traumatic.

The perfectionist's unwelcome companion is pressure. The pressure and fatigue are a in no way-completing loop due to the regular want to perform perfectly. In their pursuit of excellence, perfectionists frequently forget about their private health and protection. Constant anxiety has been related to troubles in conjunction with your immune device, digestion, and brilliant of sleep.

When a perfectionist's efforts do not pay off the way they need them to, they begin to enjoy down. The dread of in no manner being "applicable sufficient" persists however out of doors confirmation and successes. A profound feel of inadequacy and hopelessness is fostered via the continual dissatisfaction with one's non-public achievements. The downhill spiral into melancholy is improved via the not unusual contrast with an idealised photograph of oneself or others.

Self-criticism and a loss of self-compassion are commonplace amongst individuals who strive for perfection. When perfectionists make a mistake or face adversity, they will be regularly too tough on themselves, starting a vicious cycle of self-criticism. The greater they punish themselves, the greater their worry, anxiety, and disappointment develop, making it more hard to get away the cycle.

Relationships go through even as a person is a perfectionist due to the fact they tend to assignment their personal ideals onto others round them. Because in their disability to simply accept flaws in others, perfectionists regularly discover themselves on my own and at odds with others spherical them.

The dating amongst perfectionism and mental health problems is nuanced and tough. It's a self-perpetuating loop of terrible emotions fueling perfectionism, which in flip consequences in greater horrific emotions. A trade in attitude and reputation of flaws are critical for breaking out of this rut. The grip of perfectionism may be loosened and the direction to a better and extra happy life may be opened with the useful aid of studying to charge improvement above perfection, schooling self-compassion, and getting assist from cherished ones or experts.

In order to conquer perfectionism, one should take transport of that flaws are everyday and expected capabilities of the human situation. Adopting a boom mind-set and realising that errors and disasters are possibilities for getting to know and development aren't the same element as accepting failure and mediocrity. It consists of realising that setbacks are gaining knowledge of reviews in place of signs and signs of one's intrinsic price.

One of the splendid strategies to counteract perfectionism's damaging results is to gather out to others for assist. Meeting together with cherished ones or human beings in similar conditions could possibly help you experience time-venerated and reassure you that your flaws are suitable. A experience of community and statistics can boom while folks that go through with perfectionism percentage their testimonies with every exclusive.

Anxiety, stress, and unhappiness may be alleviated via difficult the faulty intellectual styles that hold them. As a stop bring about their "all-or-now not anything" mindset, perfectionists commonly generally have a tendency to view some thing a lot much less than excellent as a failure. Reframing one's questioning and taking a more purpose stance are competencies that may be found out to help alleviate tension and fear. A greater exceptional mind-set on existence is feasible if one realises that fulfillment isn't a vacation spot however instead a way fraught with obstacles.

Managing the acute feelings that perfectionism can bring forth can be aided thru training in mindfulness and strain bargain. The training of mindfulness facilitates human beings popularity at the proper proper right here and now, in place of dwelling on the past or the destiny. Stress and tension may be alleviated through practises which incorporates deep respiratory, meditation, and yoga.

It's releasing to do things with out stressful approximately how properly you're doing or trying to have an effect on every body else. Those who engage in hobbies, modern pastimes, or bodily sports record lower stages of strain and tension and a extra enjoy of internal delight, impartial of the approval of others.

When humans in the long run harm freed from their perfectionism, they regularly experience a experience of liberation and a clearer interest of who they sincerely are. Accepting one's flaws frees them to investigate greater approximately themselves and amplify their definition of "who they will be" beyond the proper of perfection.

Giving up inconceivable standards of perfection can assist people enjoy an lousy lot an lousy lot much less careworn. There's opportunity for a extra natural way of existence when tension over failing and competition to impress others take a back seat. When strain is decreased, humans are better capable of assume in truth and live resilient inside the face of adversity.

When perfectionism is about apart, it is also less difficult to cope with persistent strain. When human beings discover ways· to embody their personal strengths and weaknesses, they may address demanding conditions in greater green methods. They amplify a extra sustainable and wholesome manner of lifestyles through the usage of the usage of analyzing to set less highly-priced desires and supply themselves time and hobby.

Chapter 12: The Cost Of Perfection

Perfectionism is related to highbrow health problems like stress and fear. Constant vigilance and apprehension is probably the very last results of demanding approximately failing and seeking to live as much as not viable standards. The perception that one isn't always particular enough may be reinforced by the frustration and self-grievance that unavoidably take a look at any failure, regardless of how small. This form of unrelenting pessimism has been associated with the onset of intellectual fitness problems at the side of depression.

Perfectionism frequently leads people to adopt an all-or-no longer something mentality, wherein they view activities as both perfect or catastrophic screw ups. As a give up end result of this cognitive distortion, humans may be a whole lot a great deal less probable to have a study from their failures and more likely to avoid tough situations for worry of failing. This may additionally moreover cause perfectionists to sense stuck and unfulfilled whilst you recall that they're now not able to development in their very non-public lives.

The pursuit of perfection would possibly have unfavorable results on one's frame. Unrelenting pursuit of perfection is mounted with stepped forward cortisol tiers and disturbed sleep cycles because of the pressure and tension it reasons. This should have a cumulative effect of reducing resistance to contamination and growing susceptibility to contamination.

To alleviate their pressure, perfectionists may additionally moreover flip to awful method, collectively with binge consuming or substance abuse. The physical toll of perfectionism is exacerbated at the equal time as one's private goals for self-care and relaxation are ignored in pursuit of the pursuit of perfection.

Perfectionism can be hard in social interactions. Perfectionists might also discover it hard to shape tremendous relationships with others due to the truth they will be so targeted on challenge their nice that they may be afraid of being criticised or rejected if they fall brief. Depression, anxiety, and special highbrow health troubles may also additionally boom because of multiplied isolation and loneliness.

The effects of perfectionism on one's emotional and bodily nicely-being are tremendous and some distance-reaching. Self-recognition, self-compassion, and the braveness to simply accept imperfection as inherent to the human enjoy are important for liberation from perfectionism. The stresses of perfectionism may be reduced and a happier, extra exciting life may be done by using adopting a more balanced and realistic attitude.

Developing self-compassion is important at the direction to letting pass of perfectionism. Self-compassion includes giving oneself the identical empathy, tolerance, and encouragement that one may provide to a friend in a similar situation. Accepting one's personal fallibility and the inevitable necessity of gaining knowledge of from one's mistakes is vital.

A perfectionist's inner critic may be combated and self-judgment changed with reputation if she or he adopts a greater compassionate attitude within the direction of themselves. They can forestall being so tough on themselves for falling short of unachievable beliefs and start celebrating even the smallest of victories. A stronger connection to oneself and others can be fostered thru adopting this new mindset, which conjures up a more balanced and loving approach to improvement.

One of the keys to overcoming perfectionism is mastering to set cheap desires and expectancies. People can recognition on what topics most to them rather than looking to acquire perfection in every place of their lives. By that specialize in a doable huge form of sports, human beings can avoid turning into overwhelmed or burned out.

Negative impacts of perfectionism may be mitigated with the resource of training relaxation, stress cut price, and mindfulness. Stress can be reduced, emotional nicely-being extra, and a more optimistic thoughts-set on existence fostered thru regular use of meditation, yoga, or one-of-a-kind mindfulness techniques.

Part of this approach entails seeing setbacks and errors as reading opinions. Those who war with perfectionism can also train themselves to look failures not as signs and symptoms of failure but as opportunities to increase. When humans adopt a increase mindset, they view setbacks as possibilities to improvement intellectually, emotionally, and behaviorally.

The poor results of perfectionism on one's highbrow and bodily fitness can be conquer via the improvement of self-reputation, self-compassion, inexpensive expectancies, social help, and a boom attitude. The direction to a happier, greater exciting, and properly-balanced existence is paved with the recognition of flaws and the recognition of 1's non-public and others' innate well really worth. As a end result, humans are better able to apprehend success, develop from failure, and recognize the wonders of being human.

It's commonplace for humans to enjoy a dramatic boom of their capacity to particular themselves creatively and freely as they art work through their struggles with perfectionism. By letting flow into of the call for for perfection, humans are loose to pursue their passions without traumatic approximately what others should think. As a result, they'll come into closer touch with their right selves, make bigger previously unknown talents, and find out extra meaning in lifestyles.

As the weight of perfectionism lessens, a few humans file higher simple health. Better sleep, extra strength, and a more potent immune system are surely a number of the blessings that could accrue from reducing stress and adopting healthy coping techniques. Achieving a sense of equilibrium in a unmarried's lifestyles frees up greater intellectual and physical energy for hobbies that growth normal happiness.

Conquering perfectionism is related to income in efficiency and originality in a single's strolling life. Those who strive for improvement instead of perfection are more likely to test out novel techniques and thoughts. This mental shift encourages a greater flexible and modern method to artwork, which in turn consequences in higher productivity and extended pastime pleasure.

When one character is in a feature to interrupt free of perfectionism, it usually encourages those round them to do the same. Leading with the resource of example and telling their story can encourage humans to simply accept their flaws and located their very own happiness in advance of a best global. This domino effect has the capability to make our international a higher region with the aid of the usage of helping individuals and companies take shipping of and resource each other on their character paths.

How striving for perfection influences your social lifestyles and relationships

Various types of dating perfectionism exist. Those who suffer from perfectionism once in a while enjoy persistent feelings of dissatisfaction and sadness due to their disability to just accept flaws in themselves and their partners. The want for perfection can cause a important thoughts-set wherein the target turns into overly targeted on their associate's shortcomings. Because they fear about falling quick in their idealized selves, perfectionists may avoid getting involved in romantic relationships truly.

Perfectionists may not be able to be open and real in their relationships because of a fear of being judged or rejected. They may additionally repress their emotions and thoughts because of the fact they fear that their loved ones will abandon them inside the event that they display their vulnerabilities. The disability to unique feelings brazenly can create distance in relationships.

Feeling inadequate and prefer one has to continuously have a look at oneself to others are not unusual consequences of perfectionism in social conditions. When a perfectionist feels strain to assignment a perfect image of oneself to others, social engagements can emerge as traumatic instead of amusing. To prevent the possibility of failing to stay as an awful lot as their very personal exacting standards, perfectionists may additionally additionally withdraw from others and isolate themselves.

The manner an man or woman system and reacts to complaint and remarks will also be triggered by way of way in their tendency closer to perfectionism. Those who attempt for perfection are more likely to take criticism in my view, in preference to as a chance to enhance. They also can end up protective and proof in the direction of trade as a give up result, lowering their capability for growth and improvement.

In addition, perfectionists are at risk of burnout and pressure because of their consistent efforts to fall short of their personal beliefs. The emotional and behavioral consequences of this heightened pressure on relationships and social interactions may be unfavorable.

Self-popularity and a willingness to observe prolonged-held views are vital for overcoming perfectionism. Understanding the terrible effects of perfectionism on one's private and social existence can be notably aided with the aid of the usage of way of remedy and the encouragement of loved ones. Healthy, great relationships and a extra exciting social existence may be the quit end result of learning to include vulnerability, practicing self-compassion, and realising that faults are an inevitable a part of being human. Keep in thoughts that sizeable friendships are primarily based no longer on the reason of perfection but on popularity, empathy, and expertise.

Transformative shifts in relationships and social interactions may be professional as humans begin to address their perfectionistic impulses. By amusing their necessities, they make room for real conversations and extensive relationships with others.

Having the functionality to empathise and recognize one's associate is facilitated by means of manner of cultivating a addiction of vulnerability and self-compassion. They stop being so difficult on themselves and others they care about, and begin celebrating their differences. A more potent emotional connection and a extra encouraging and enriching environment for personal development are the results of this newfound popularity.

Learning to take grievance in a healthful way can assist perfectionists extend as people and as a part of social groups. They shift their mind-set on failure and start to appearance it as an possibility to develop. Because in their growth thoughts-set, they're capable of alternate and develop as a couple, which strengthens their bonds and makes them more resilient to adversity.

The social benefits of letting cross of perfectionism encompass greater actual interactions with pals and coworkers. They are liberated to be themselves in social conditions for the reason that they not feel the pressure to constantly initiate or stay as an lousy lot as irrational expectancies. This allows them to develop tremendous relationships with others at the concept of commonplace floor and appreciation.

Getting over perfectionism furthermore makes it an awful lot much less scary to position yourself to be had and meet new people because of the fact you fear much less about being judged or rejected. They sense tons much less stress to act in a super way and feature more self guarantee even as interacting with others.

Improved intellectual fitness is a not unusual give up result of lessening perfectionism-associated stress and tension. Learning to in reality accept and love oneself effects in greater happiness and internal serenity, which in flip improves one's interactions with others.

One gain of jogging to conquer perfectionism is the capability for progressed non-public business corporation organization and flourishing in a single's interpersonal relationships. Moreover, letting flow of perfectionism should have an impact on their social interactions in the following techniques:

When humans prevent residing on their private failings, they're better in a position to narrate to the ones of others. Because of their advanced capability for empathy, they're capable of shape more potent bonds with the humans in their lives.

Authenticity fosters connection as it permits humans to be themselves in social settings, flaws and all. They revel in greater related to others and function a extra sense of belonging once they permit down their facade of excellence.

The capability to persevere through marital problems grows as people lighten up their necessities of perfection. They do now not deal with every argument as even though it were the give up of the arena, but as an opportunity as a everyday part of any dating that may be used as a training 2d.

Taking satisfaction in the right here and now's difficult for perfectionists, who have an inclination to recognition at the beyond or the destiny. They can higher appreciate the human beings of their lives and characteristic fun with the pleasure of shared studies through the usage of simply residing in the 2d.

When people feel lots much less threatened via manner of others' reviews, they will be much more likely to talk their minds and specific their sentiments brazenly. Better listening and conversation abilities emerge alongside improved self-popularity, main to greater superb and together supportive relationships.

Perfectionists want to preserve company only with folks who seem to degree as an awful lot as their exacting standards. But if they may be able to permit pass of their want for perfection, they will be able to form sizeable connections with human beings from all walks of existence, increasing their horizons and deepening their social studies.

Putting apart ideals of perfection frees people to revel in the blessings of their interactions with others. Changing one's mind-set to one of appreciation may likely enhance one's outlook on life and increase happiness.

Studies on how striving for perfection can inhibit innovation and modern thinking

Studies have related striving for perfection to feelings of hysteria and self-doubt. These horrific emotions are number one roadblocks to specific perception. Fear of complaint may reason humans to avoid taking risks and alternatively pursue attempted-and-actual strategies, limiting their capacity to give you particular thoughts and glowing techniques to vintage issues.

Perfectionists are often their very personal worst critics, always seeking out a few component incorrect with their paintings. Fear of failure or searching stupid can save you you from completing tasks and taking location, because self-grievance can lure you in an countless cycle of transform. Because of this, particular idea is hindered and the revolutionary method toilets down.

Interestingly, research suggests that places wherein humans are recommended to fear too much about making mistakes have a propensity to stifle their imaginations. However, creativity and new thoughts flourish in settings wherein mistakes are traditional or maybe endorsed as a part of the instructional system. Creating an surroundings wherein taking dangers is rewarded makes human beings more open to attempting new topics, which in flip sparks greater innovation.

Academics and experts pressure the price of a increase mind-set as a way of preventing the destructive influences of a pursuit of perfection on modern output. In this way of questioning, one accepts the opportunity of developing and strengthening one's talents thru check and exercise. Freeing oneself from the confines of perfectionism and embracing the boundless ability of imperfection requires a shift in mindset from failure to achievement.

The adverse results of perfectionism bypass a protracted manner past the vicinity of human creativeness and originality. The occurrence of perfectionistic perspectives can generate a toxic surroundings that stifles the loose go together with the go together with the glide of mind and hampers collective trouble-solving in collaborative settings like groups and groups.

Those who attempt for perfection may be overly critical of the work of others, developing an environment wherein anyone is on element and seeking out to defend themselves. This prevents human beings from freely sharing thoughts and operating together, this is important for developing ground-breaking discoveries. Team contributors are an awful lot tons much less willing to offer novel, risky ideas that could result in exercise-changing breakthroughs when they worry about being judged harshly for his or her efforts.

However, encouraging originality and sparkling thoughts calls for cultivating an environment in which people feel stable sufficient to take risks and communicate their minds without fear of reprimand. Innovative answers to difficult stressful conditions are much more likely to emerge in settings in which ideas can bloom and groups can construct upon every other's contributions.

Perfectionism has repercussions past the place of work, which incorporates at the manner societies view and pursue increase and innovation. People can be a good deal much less likely to attempt a few component new or chance failure inside the occasion that they accept as true with society expects them to do flawlessly or place too much price on their achievements proper away. Individuals may be dissuaded from taking risks that may boom human facts and era because of problems of being judged harshly for making mistakes.

Educators and business organisation leaders alike have to make cultivating a growth attitude a top priority in the occasion that they want to create an environment that rewards unique notion. Individuals can growth resilience and tenacity within the face of adversity with the aid of using being taught to view setbacks as valuable mastering possibilities. If you need to free human beings's imaginations and assist them attain their entire ability, try cultivating an environment wherein they may be praised for their efforts, their interest, and their willingness to discover in vicinity of judged in simple terms on their effects.

Moreover, encouraging pass-disciplinary paintings can stimulate creativity via exposing people to new processes of questioning. Collaboration between experts from numerous domain names regularly results in groundbreaking new discoveries. This mingling of perspectives can assist people assume beyond the container, that is critical for solving difficult stressful situations.

Chapter 13: Overcoming Perfectionism

To get started, simply sit together alongside your mind for a while. Think about times at the same time as your need for perfection has introduced on tension or averted you from taking vital steps. Consider how your need for perfection affected your emotions and movements and why you felt that way. During this time, it's miles vital to be gentle and sort to yourself, reminding yourself that it's miles adequate to be incorrect.

Keeping a pocket ebook that you detail your perfectionist thoughts and feelings is probably a beneficial interest. Jot down the times below which your perfectionism manifests itself, as well as the thoughts and feelings that accompany it. Look for repetitions on your thoughts, which incorporates the want for out of doors approval or putting unrealistically immoderate goals for yourself. You can begin to question the ones behavior once you recognize they exist.

Reframing your inner speak is a drastically effective technique. Stop and take stock if you discover your self thinking too especially of your self. Self-compassion consists of being type to your self in choice to harshly judging your imperfections. Keep in mind that mistakes are an fundamental part of the learning and development method. Substitute bad self-talk with excessive splendid affirmations and communicate to yourself with the same compassion you'll show to a chum in want.

Seeking out errors is a few different manner to schooling accepting them. Intentionally provide room for errors and purpose for small, possible dreams. Try some trouble new, even though it's best a ultra-modern recipe or a cutting-edge interest. Accept yourself in that you are in your reading and be thrilled along with your efforts, win or lose.

Mindfulness is the functionality of listening to one's internal memories without passing judgement on them. Recognise that you're having mind of perfectionism without giving in to them. Mindfulness permits you to grow to be more in music collectively with your internal experience, allowing you to reply to conditions with greater deliberation in choice to reactive haste.

Check your assumptions in competition to real activities. Ask yourself if you're putting expectations which is probably every cheap and ability at the same time as you find yourself questioning that the whole thing need to be exquisite. Think approximately how your pursuit of perfection impacts your happiness and the fine of your relationships. You do now not want to be incredible to reap achievement or to be general with the aid of manner of others, so that you need to look for examples that display this.

Take element in pastimes that assist you feel better approximately your self and your price to the area. Appreciate yourself with the useful resource of recognizing your dispositions and achievements, no matter how insignificant they'll appear. Put yourself in the business enterprise of remarkable, encouraging those who will now not decide or criticize you for who you are.

You also can moreover experience infection or setbacks as you keep your quest to confront perfectionistic ideals. The dependancy of perfectionism is difficult to stop considering that it is so deeply ingrained. Keep in thoughts that transformation is a adventure and that you may anticipate usaand downs along the direction.

Realize that striving for perfection is a losing conflict which can sap your electricity and leisure. Instead, you must cause to do your exceptional and understand at the same time as mediocrity is appropriate. Giving up the pursuit of perfection can help you experience greater snug and at peace.

Regularly have interaction in acts of self-compassion. Be as affected person and compassionate with yourself as you'll be with a near friend or family member. Keep in mind that making errors is inevitable and that it in no manner lowers your fee as a man or women.

Do topics that inspire you to anticipate out of doors the sphere and test. Let pass of perfectionist beliefs and dive headfirst into the fun of experimentation. Relax your seriousness and attention on having fun without annoying about the final results of your innovative or athletic endeavours.

Find a network of folks that can relate to your perfectionism and assist you thru it. Finding a community of folks who proportion your pursuits and views can be a great supply of assist and idea to your direction to self-splendor and private development.

Seek help from a therapist or counsellor if you feel that your ideals of perfection are firmly ingrained and are affecting your life. Their advice and suggest can be beneficial as you face these limitations and make progress closer to a more powerful body of thoughts.

Keep in mind that it is suitable to have setbacks even as you keep for your route of self-discovery and improvement. It takes time, endurance, and paintings to change prolonged-held attitudes and behavior. Remember that boom isn't usually linear, and be type to your self at the same time as you come across setbacks. No recollect how massive or tiny, improvement is normally welcome.

Reframing bad thoughts

In order to free oneself from the guidelines of perfectionism, cognitive-behavioral techniques can be used to reframe terrible thoughts and foster self-compassion. Constant self-complaint, fear of failure, and an unachievable pursuit of perfection are all symptoms of perfectionism, which can have a crippling effect on one's intellectual fitness.

Having a super draw close on one's non-public consciousness is important. The capability to recognize unfavourable concept patterns and see the onset of perfectionism is important.

The basis for development and transformation is laid while the ones conduct are appeared with out criticism. A person's capacity to project their very very very own awful beliefs starts with an boom in self-recognition.

Mind-converting cognitive reorganisation is one such technique. This requires wondering critically approximately the arguments for and towards pessimistic conclusions. Is this notion supported via goal proof? Have there been times as soon as I haven't been satisfactory, but I nevertheless valued myself as a person? These are the kinds of questions we're able to ask ourselves while we are confronted with self-important mind like "I need to typically excel or I'm nugatory."

Negative mind are not right now challenged; instead, human beings learn how to take a look at them with out becoming emotionally invested in them. Visualise your mind as clouds floating thru in the sky, accepting their presence without turning into caught up in them. This lets in you to step again from harsh self-grievance and make room for self-compassion.

Self-compassion is an essential tool within the combat in opposition to perfectionism. When you training self-compassion, you display yourself the identical compassion that you might supply to a close pal. Realising that flaws are inherent to human nature and that no individual is right is critical. Self-compassion allows us to realize our frailties and shortcomings in the face of adversity with out resorting to harsh self-criticism. This encourages resiliency and a more first rate outlook on self-improvement.

Self-compassion is the conscious cultivation of self-kindness, giant humanism, and recognition. Instead than beating ourselves up for falling brief of impossible dreams, we've got amusing our development and receive our price. Understanding that we are all human and hassle to flaws lets in us bond over our not unusual humanity and not unusual humanity with others.

As an added bonus, effective self-affirmations can be effective weapons in competition to horrific inner monologue. A healthful and wonderful self-image can be fostered via crafting first-rate affirmations approximately one's abilities, tendencies, and fee. Regular use of these affirmations allow you to internalise their useful messages and mitigate the awful impacts of striving for perfection.

Self-compassion entails listening to our inner communicate and reacting to ourselves with kindness and empathy. The extra we have interplay in this addiction, the extra we are capable of get higher from setbacks and create a extra grounded experience of self-worth this is untethered from unrealistic expectancies of perfection.